Thrivin' Now!

Achieve Success, Build Wealth, and *Be Happy* In the Post-Covid World

Dallas E. Stiles, Jr.

Thrivin' Now!-Achieve Success, Build Wealth, and Be Happy In the Post-Covid World

Published by Thrivin LLC

Website: thrivinllc.com

Email: thrivindude@yahoo.com

Library of Congress Cataloging-In-Publication Data:

ISBN (Paperback) 978-0-578-29022-5

ISBN (eBook) 978-0-578-29023-2

Contents

Introduction

Thrivin' Now!-After the Pandemic

Congratulations! You've made it to the post-pandemic world. At least that's how I view things as I sit here at the beginning of 2022 putting the final touches on this book.

The pandemic has shaped who we are during the past two years. While some people have been conditioned to not let Covid go, and there will be brief periods of panic as new variants emerge, the reality is, death rates are now very low and falling further. It's likely anti-virals, past and present, will ultimately be proven to be effective and hopefully a lot safer than the current "vaccines." I hope these treatments will finally reassure the remaining fearful folks out there that they can take their masks off and move on with their lives.

What's your game plan when covid is no longer a big deal?

For almost two years, we have been instructed how to act and live. When Covid fades away, the question is, what will you do with yourself after you finally jettison your mask and start shaking hands with people again?

No doubt, the more restrictive blue states and world governments will likely be slow and generally reluctant to relinquish the freedoms they've sequestered over the past two years (see Canada as I write this in early 2022!). But eventually, in the next months or maybe year, the masks, social distancing, and vaccine passports will likely fade away. Hopefully for good!

Thrivin' Now-after the pandemic...

While this book is being published during Covid, it's not about the pandemic per se. It discusses how we can each successfully move forward and thrive personally now that this nightmarish, Orwellian period is hopefully receding into the rearview mirror.

Life and, in particular, many aspects of the working world, have changed in some fairly significant ways during the pandemic. To the nimble and astute, will likely go the rewards. **This book highlights several ways *you* can take advantage of this new world to achieve success in your career, build wealth, and sustain real happiness.**

Power is tilting to the worker.

While many companies are still grappling with this new world, including tech darlings like Google and Facebook who are frantically trying to herd all their worker bees back into their cubicles, the reality is an axis shift in how work is conducted has occurred, and the power relationship between many employers and their employees has changed, at least for the foreseeable future. **How do *you* take advantage of that in order to maximize *your* potential?**

I started writing this book decades ago with the fairly straightforward thought that it would be about helping folks early in their career climb the corporate ladder. At the time, I was in my early 30's myself and had some success climbing said ladder, becoming a corporate VP at the age of 32. Initially, my thought for the title of this book way back then was "VP by 33" because it fit my situation at the time and, well, "VP" and "33" rhymed!

While I've worked on this book on and off over the last several years, incorporating additional topics that now cover the full scope of a career, the pandemic really lit a fire for me to finish this book with some urgency given the changes I have observed unfolding over the past two years. I am now finishing this book after exiting the "working for someone else" phase of my career, which I call my emancipation. More on that topic in a later chapter.

With the passage of a few decades, and the last two years of unparalleled upheaval due to Covid, the scope of this book has changed from focusing just on early career advice, to a broader focus of living your entire working career to the fullest, achieving success, building wealth, and achieving the ultimate goal of enjoying sustained happiness.

What's most important in *your* life?

A successful career can certainly help contribute to sustained happiness, but it's not the be all/end all. In this book, I try to outline the tools and strategies I've developed over my life to help on the quest towards the dual objectives of being successful and building wealth while not sacrificing the most important objective, personal happiness. Given many aspects of working life have been altered during the pandemic, I've tried to flag those changes and have provided my thoughts on what these mean in terms of making choices and leveraging opportunities in the future.

I've had my share of challenges and internal struggles, including some described in this book, but I've lived a really happy life with a fair share of career success that has given me a lot of personal satisfaction. While I've certainly been blessed with many things over the years, I've learned there are fundamental tools and approaches that can be utilized by just about anyone to build a successful career, grow wealth, and be happy while doing it.

This book is about sharing the practical, actionable things I've learned and incorporated into my daily life with the hope that you will find at least some of these approaches helpful in improving your life as well.

Chapter 1

Why This Book is Worth Your Attention

There are countless books giving advice on every imaginable life topic with whole sections of every bookstore, both physical and online, devoted to business and career advice.

Why should you invest some of your valuable time to read my book? Because people who are interested in achieving something more in life are often looking for new insights on how to grow personally and professionally.

I place a lot more trust in whoever is telling me something if they have actually gone out and done the things they are giving advice on, it gives them more credibility than say, some academic. As it relates to the topics covered in this book, while not intending to be boastful, I've "done it:"

- Achieved career success as a senior executive with several private and multi-national public companies.
- Built personal wealth.
- Most importantly, figured out how to be very happy almost all of the time. Having had a successful marriage, now going on 35 years, no doubt helped me a lot on all of the above.

I did it and so can *you!*
Consistent use of the tools I describe in this book really helped me through my working career. My objectives with this book are to provide you with useful insights and real tangible ways to not only manage your career successfully but also to manage the fruits of your labor (growing your wealth) and, most importantly, to live a happy, fulfilling life.

How to get the most out of this book

This book is organized somewhat chronologically as one would typically encounter things during their life and career. Included are a number of specific, actionable approaches you can incorporate into you own life to:

- Establish goals
- Manage stress
- Maintain life balance
- Position yourself for success
- Build wealth
- Most importantly - **be happy**

Pick the parts of this book that are most helpful for you

While it's my goal that this entire book is useful to you, the following provides a thumbnail for the different sections of the book in the event there is a particular topic you want to jump to for immediate information:

Is your life in balance? Goal setting & your Personal Inventory

The first chapters are focused on habits and techniques I figured out early on in my life to help manage stress and live a more balanced life.

As I detail later, as a kid, and to some extent, as a young adult, I was a big worrier and, from time to time, dealt with anxiety. These early chapters detail how I approach goal setting and describe a few of the key mental tools and habits I developed over the years that I call "My Personal Inventory" and "My Mantra."

These tools and habits have helped me think through what was going on in my life at any point in time in a rationale, organized way.

Over the years, they have really allowed me to manage many things at the same time without getting overwhelmed by them, or life in general.

These tools and habits have absolutely been key for me in achieving success. Learning to be able to juggle lots of professional and personal things at the same time without excessive stress helped me to live a happy and balanced existence. I am hopeful these tools will be useful to you as well.

Changes after the pandemic: how can they benefit you?

The middle set of chapters focus on career, starting with figuring out what to do with your life and how to effectively navigate your career ladder. Included are some observations and insights into several of the changes in modern work the pandemic accelerated. These include whole new career paths such as skipping college altogether and starting a business, or maximizing your career on the more traditional "go to college and work for someone else" path, or beginning a slash career.

Our two sons are very representative of a few of these trends. One has an expanding slash career (this is defined as one where you have multiple jobs and income streams that each feed into an overarching longer term career objective). My other son dropped out of college after his freshman year to focus on building the music production and management business he started when he was 14.

Observing their experiences, I've seen first hand how these new types of career options are evolving and the real opportunities that exist today to make a wider range of career choices compared to when I was figuring out what I wanted to do in life.

Does stress adversely impact you?

Regardless of how your career unfolds, stress is always there. I've included a chapter on ways I found helpful to manage and channel stress in productive, rather than destructive ways.

Career inflection points

I thrived on the more traditional corporate career path, and I offer insights on what I call "career inflection points" that will hopefully provide some ideas to those navigating the corporate jungle. These inflection points, when observed and acted on properly, can dramatically accelerate your career trajectory.

Negotiating...securing your best deal

Wrapping up this middle portion of the book, I provide some tips on negotiating your best deal. The higher you rise on the ladder, the more you will need to be savvy and thoughtful in negotiating all aspects of the arrangement between you and your employer. This of course, includes not only your salary but also a whole host of other compensation elements you probably have not encountered earlier in your career such as stock options, restricted stock units, and/or equity. It also includes insight into the important but often overlooked topic of negotiating an equitable separation when you and your employer inevitably decide to part ways in the future.

"You Incorporated:" building real wealth over your career

One of the things that just blows me away is how many people of all walks of life, including many really smart professionals I know, do not know the basics, or simply lack the confidence, to manage their money and build wealth themselves, without paying someone else to do it for them.

To help, I've included several chapters later in the book under the "You Incorporated" heading that explain these basics and provide specific ways to put yourself on a path to successfully managing your money and build significant wealth. All without needing to get an MBA or paying a financial advisor a dime.

While not intending to give specific investment advice, these chapters provide an outline, in simple language with examples of how you can successfully build significant wealth over the course of your career, manage your investments efficiently, and achieve performance that is as good as most professionally managed investment portfolios. I know that may sound impossible, but it's absolutely true and I'll provide references to studies that prove this is the case.

This basic knowledge on how to build wealth is a skill that is critically lacking in many successful professional people. So even if you are well on your way to having a great career and paying someone else to manage your investments, you should find this portion of the book valuable. These tools can be implemented at any stage of your life but due to the miracle of compounding, which I discuss later in the book, the sooner the better! I've ended this section with a chapter showing how you can objectively evaluate, based on recent market performance, if your financial advisor is earning the money you're paying them.

Are you curious about crypto??

I have also included a bonus chapter on the crypto world of blockchains. I am convinced these are transformational technologies akin to the advent of electricity and the internet.

At first glance, it can be very confusing to understand the crypto world. Having spent a considerable amount of time myself learning the basics over the past few years, I explain blockchain technology here in an easily digestible way for you to understand the key terms, so you can hopefully start wrapping your brain around the massive potential that exists.

According to earthweb.com's Thomas McGovern, as of early 2022, it's estimated that only 3.9% of the world's population have owned crypto, so it's still very early days. While very risky and volatile, blockchains will transform many large industries. The sooner you understand this technology, the better.

Do you ever want to stop working full time for someone else?

Of course you do! Chapter 16 focuses on what I call "emancipation," which I define as freeing yourself from the "working for someone else full time" phase of your career. I differentiate this from "retirement" because retirement connotes stopping work altogether.

One thing emancipation and retirement both have in common though, and I am living this reality currently, is that it's important to carefully think about and plan what you want to do when you stop working for someone else, or stop working altogether. Abruptly ending what you've spent the majority of your waking hours doing for your entire adult life and assuming not having something to fill that void will all work out ok is frequently a recipe for problems.

In this chapter, I detail some of the thought processes I went through in determining if I could emancipate (from a financial perspective), and as importantly, what did I want to do with my life when I emancipated. The latter question took many months longer than the first one to figure out. As of this writing, I am 11 months into emancipation and honestly, I've not looked back with regret for one nanosecond…so far!

Be a Learning Creature: check out the suggested references

Following the conclusion of this book, I've listed some books, podcasts, websites, and other references I have found to be educational, thought-provoking, and entertaining. Hopefully, some of these will be interesting to you and will spark further investigation into one or more of the topics covered on your never-ending journey as a learning creature.

While there are always many challenges we each face, I believe there has never been a better time for: starting your career, starting a business, making course corrections during your career, or creating your plan to emancipate. A successful career is gratifying and building wealth provides security and opportunities but, to me, the overarching life objective is to maximize ***your sustained happiness.***

Important!

This book is intended to provide some useful information and hopefully, a little education. It details my thoughts and opinions on the topics I cover based on my experiences. It is not in any way intended as financial advice, nor as giving recommendations to make specific investments. I am not a financial advisor in any way, shape, or form.

As I note throughout this book, one of the keys to being successful, building wealth, and being happy is, you need to be a learning creature. That means seeking out multiple points of view and approaches to accomplishing what you seek to do. Use the information in this book as one point of reference and research others, then make *your* own decisions. **You own You**.

Chapter 2

Do You Want to be a Millionaire?

From a pretty early age, I would tell just about anyone who would listen that, "I want to be a millionaire by the age of 40." While not a unique goal, I don't know when or how it got planted in my young brain, but it certainly was lodged in my mine before I was 10. Looking back, it was the first durable goal I ever set, even if I didn't have a road map for many years to get me to that destination.

In grad school, as I was preparing to start my first full time job, the first big long term career goal I set was to become a Vice President by the age of 33. My dad, while having had a successful career working for the same Fortune 500 company his entire working life, ultimately rising to becoming a corporate officer had, nonetheless, never achieved the "VP" title. For me, to go a step beyond, at least from a title standpoint, what my dad had accomplished was important. Why by the age of 33? It's simple: it rhymed with VP. Plus, achieving this level by that age seemed doable. So "VP by 33" became my initial career goal.

Many years ago, when I first started writing this book, my original intent was to write only about the quest to achieve these two goals: becoming a VP by 33, and being a millionaire by the age of 40 because, ultimately, I did achieve both of these goals (spoiler alert!).

I am now quite a bit older and recently stopped working for someone else full time. One of my primary goals during this first year of emancipation is to complete this book, focusing not just on the two early goals noted above, but also to provide some ideas and insights that cover the full scope of your working career.

I worked in business for roughly 35 years leading the sales and marketing efforts for several private and global public companies. Over that time, I have learned a number of things that I will boil down to a basic set of simple ways to improve your life with special attention to improving your career while, ideally, not burning yourself out and/or churning through 3 marriages and/or broken relationships with your kids. Throughout the book, I'll flag the synopsis of these key points as "Life Hacks."

My background

For context, let me tell you a little about myself, what I am and what I am not. The options, as I saw them, when I graduated high school way back in 1980, were pretty black and white. If you wanted any shot at having any success in life, you needed a college degree. I grew up in Ohio and graduated from The Ohio State University with a BSBA in marketing. I followed that with an MBA from Case Western Reserve University.

While completing my MBA, I joined a plastics packaging company as a summer marketing research intern. Several years after graduation, I advanced to the position of Vice President of Sales and Marketing at this company. A few years later, I accepted a position as Vice President of Sales and Marketing at a company in the electronics industry near Chicago.

Over the course of my career, I have managed the commercial organizations at the director, VP, or Senior VP level for several multi-billion dollar global public companies. Recently, I made the transition from working full time for someone else to writing this book, consulting, and working "fractionally," a newer term, which means I do what I want when I want, lending my experience to companies on a project or interim basis…and so far, it's awesome!

Critically important to my success and sanity is that I have had the great fortune of being married for 35 years. We have two sons who are both grown and beginning their careers. My sons' more recent experiences and career objectives, briefly touched on in Chapter 1, have been really enlightening to me. They highlight the dramatic changes in opportunities and options that exist now compared to when I started my career...more to come on these topics later in the book.

I am not a psychologist, a psychiatrist, an analyst, an academic, a teacher, a financial advisor, or an ivy league blue blood (to paraphrase a Seinfeld line, "not that there's anything wrong with those things!"). I'm not a genius, though I sometimes explain to my wife and sons that I am.

The bottom line is I am a pretty regular guy who grew up as part of a family of 6 in a middle class suburb and attended public school. At this point in my life, I have achieved most of the significant goals that I've set out to do. The ways I have accomplished these are highlighted in this book and if I can do it, so can just about anyone.

I hope you will find this book valuable because I am like many of you. I grew up, went to school, and went to work. I started working at the age of 13 delivering papers and working in fast food. Despite the stereotypes of some "woke folks" today, I did not have any special privileges, and I would wager the poverty my parents rose out of surpasses almost all folks living in the US today. I obtained every job on my own without family help or any special connections that I didn't develop myself.

Life Hack #1: Many of you will compete against individuals with special privileges and connections...welcome to the real world that has and always will exist. A "victim" mentality will not help you...to the contrary, it will do the opposite. You can cry about life not always being fair, or you can accept that reality and do something about it by learning more, adding new in-demand skills, and out-working and out-hustling your competition for the benefit of yourself and your family. You Own You.

My hope is this book helps you level the playing field so you can achieve *your* full potential, both professionally and personally.

I have tried to keep this book straight and to the point, to make key insights clear, and to provide examples in a concise way. Some of the things that got me off my butt to allocate the time to write this book include seeing not only the upheaval caused by the pandemic but also the early career fits and starts of young folks I know personally, as well as people I've worked with struggling with a job loss later in their career. This book is dedicated to them in hopes that some of the thoughts are useful in helping their careers and lives move in a positive, fulfilling direction.

Chapter 3

Goals: Making a Contract with Yourself

The power of a written goal

A 1979 Harvard survey of a class of MBA students asked "have you set clear, written goals for your future and made plans to accomplish them." The survey results showed 3% of the class had written goals and plans, 13% had unwritten goals, and 84% had no goals at all. Ten years later, a review of the survey respondents showed that the 3% who had written goals and plans in college had earned 10 times as much as the other 97% of the participants combined!

A more recent study by psychology professor Dr. Gail Matthews at the Dominican University in California showed in a survey of 267 people from around the world and from all walks of life that achieving your goals increased by 42% if they were written down and the odds of achievement increased even more if you shared those written goals with someone close to you.

One of the most important and powerful things I learned during my sophomore year at Ohio State was in an Organizational Behavior class taught by Dr. Kim. The first day of class, our professor asked us each to take out a piece of paper and write down the following:

"In this class I will achieve the following grade for the quarter:_____."

A simple statement to be sure, but what Dr. Kim was enlightening the class about was the importance of goal setting…and the almost magical power of a written goal. Instead of the typical opening class session of going over the course syllabus, Dr. Kim was essentially asking us to think about and *create a written contract with ourselves* on what we expected to achieve in this course. Dr Kim proceeded to explain, with some persuasive statistics, the power of written goals vs. non-written goals…better known as wishful thinking.

This concept stuck with me more than most of the other things I learned in college (certainly more than programing FORTRAN with punch cards…yes, I'm that old!). Over the years, I've come to believe that carefully thinking about and writing down your goals is fundamental to success in your personal and business life. I know this habit has been hugely beneficial in my own life.

Life Hack #2: Whatever significant things you want to accomplish in life…both personally and professionally… your odds of success will be greatly multiplied if you write down the goal first!

Graduate goals

When I graduated from Ohio State, I had four major goals that I wrote down prior to graduation, which I cover at various points in this book:

1. First, I wanted to quit smoking…I had become hooked on Marlboros during the course of four years of too many all nighters cramming for tests as well as trolling the legendary High Street bars with friends. I made up my mind I would quit smoking the day after graduation.

2. Second, I wanted to land a job in marketing, not sales. At that time, I had a stereotypical view of sales as cold calling and peddling, and I wanted to be on the more "sophisticated" side of marketing doing research, advertising, and publicity.

3. Third, I wanted to become a Vice President by the time I was 33 as that seemed like a stretching, but doable timeframe.

4. And finally, I wanted to be a millionaire by the time I was 40. Again, this seemed like a big stretch at the time, but this goal had been with me so long, I had to stick with it.

Smoking and trajectory

It is said that one of the hardest drug habits to break is tobacco. I started smoking in college for the same poor reasons others do. My friends did it. It looked cool. It was pleasurable while drinking in a bar. It helped me stay awake and served as a kind of crazy reward mechanism when I studied. All these are great excuses for what, in every case, is just a really stupid and potentially deadly decision.

As described above, I decided I would quit smoking the day after I graduated from Ohio State. Of course, my actual graduation day involved celebrating by consuming mass quantities of beer and at least a few packs of smokes. In my bleary haze the following morning, while filling up my car with gas for the 2 hour drive back to my parents' house, I purchased a new pack of cigarettes without even thinking.

When I got back in the car, pack of Marlboro Reds in hand, I realized my mistake. I had hit one of the handful of important crossroads we each encounter in our life that will have a big impact on our future (more on "inflection points" later in the book): do I rationalize, "oh well, I bought this new pack, I might as well smoke them and quit tomorrow," or do I do the much harder thing and get my ass out of the car, throw the pack in the garbage can, and proceed with my original goal?

> **Life Hack #3: When confronted with an "inflection point" decision, usually the easy decision is the wrong one! Conversely, almost always, the harder (which is also usually the ethically/morally right) decision is the correct path to take.**

We encounter these decisions on the things in our life that vex us until we ultimately make the right decision, or we die conflicted never addressing the issue. Smoking, overeating, not exercising, or even writing a book…all of these come down to making a decision on a given day to change the road we are on…addressing each of these issues comes down to a simple but very difficult thing; **making the decision to change**. And then sticking with that decision to change, day after day, until the change becomes the norm and a habit.

We all battle various things like this in one way or another. I made the right decision on smoking: I *did* get my ass out of my 1976 Chrysler Cordoba (with worn Corinthian leather seats), threw the pack away, and have not smoked a cigarette since August 30, 1984. But the battle continues with other issues that are life goals of mine. The ongoing issue of striving to improve is one of the many things that makes life challenging *and* rewarding.

I'm far from perfect, but I have concluded that achieving important objectives in life comes down to one simple thing; you have to START!!! Or as Nike so aptly puts it "Just Do It!"

- The hardest page in writing a book is the first page.
- The hardest day of an exercise program is the first day.
- The hardest day to stop (fill in the blank…smoking, drinking, using drugs, etc) is the first time you encounter the opportunity to *not* do it.

Once you get into the habit of any of these things, it becomes easier and easier with each passing day. Smoking is a prime example, it's really tempting to start smoking again for a long time, certainly for many months after quitting, but after some time passes, you just don't think about it anymore.

What do you want to accomplish *right now*?

If you really want to do something, make a contract with yourself with a specific written goal that you can measure yourself against. Here are some simple examples:

- I will lose 10 pounds by December 1

- I will learn 3 songs on the guitar by Christmas
- I will save $5,000 for my retirement in 2022
- I will finish writing my book *Thrivin' Now!* by April, 2022
- I will take my kids camping 3 times this summer

Take advantage of the truly magical power of writing down a goal that you really want to achieve. You will be amazed how frequently you will achieve it ahead of schedule…even goals that, when written, you may have thought were a big stretch to ever achieve!

Tactics: where the rubber meets the road in achieving your goals
Next, take each of your goals and below it write a reasonable way, or tactic, you will use to achieve or at least get one step closer to the goal. **This is the key element that connects your current life to your desired future state after actually achieving your goal!**

Be thoughtful and realistic about setting your tactics. For more complex goals you might need multiple tactics, but for this example we'll keep it simple with one tactic for each goal:

GOAL-I will lose 10 pounds by December 1
TACTIC-I will eliminate second helpings and desserts Monday-Friday each week and measure my weight each Monday morning to monitor progress towards the goal.

GOAL-I will learn 3 songs on the guitar by Christmas
TACTIC-I will practice for 1 hour each Saturday and Sunday after the kids go to bed.

GOAL-I will save $5,000 for my retirement in 2022
TACTIC-I will set up automatic deposit from my weekly paycheck for $100/week into an S&P 500 Index fund (more on the importance of setting up automatic investments later in the book).

GOAL-I will complete writing my book Thrivin' Now by April, 2022
TACTIC-To avoid impacting time with family, I will work on the book for at least 1 hour per night while traveling on business.

GOAL-I will take my kids camping 3 times this summer
TACTIC-I will book the 3 camping dates by May 1.

Don't put it off...do it!
And then do it again the next day, and then again the next day. Figure out a reasonably objective way to get after your goals and just do it. Some goals, like quitting drugs or alcohol can be an all or nothing proposition where outside help is also required. But things like learning a new skill, or doing something like writing a book can come down to just coming up with a creative way of setting aside the time to make it happen....**but you have to start in order to achieve it!**

> **Life Hack #4:** **You control you.** ***You*** **have the power to change the trajectory of your life** **starting today**. **All you have to do is start and it's downhill from there.**

A recent study by health psychology researcher Phillippa Lally of University College London indicates it usually takes about two months...66 days to be exact...to form a new habit. The research shows it takes on average 30 days to break an existing habit.

Regardless of the exact numbers, think about how little that amount of time is in the grand scheme of your life. Such a short time to make significant changes that can affect the future of your health, wealth, and happiness! Worth trying, don't you think?

Another key element of goal setting and achievement is tracking the progress on each of your goals. You need to do a process check from time to time and sometimes course correct to ensure you are progressing in achieving everything you hope to accomplish. Otherwise, the goals may become just wishes that never happen.

Here it's important to be brutally honest with yourself. Are you on track to your satisfaction and, if not, what are you going to change to get on track? This might require an adjustment or change in your tactics. It may even require a restatement of your goal. The point is, don't kid yourself...own up to reality and go from there.

While it may not work for everyone, what I do is to take some time at the end of each year to think about my goals for the coming year. As I explain in the next chapter, I create goals centered on things I want to accomplish, usually in each of "My Personal Inventory" areas. Once these goals are set, I review them regularly and track progress weekly on a simple note on my I-phone.

For example, if it's a weight loss goal, I track my weight each week. If it's how many books I want to read in a year, I note each week if I've finished reading a book. For financial goals, I do a quarterly net worth update to see how I am progressing towards those types of goals.

The point is, while there is magic in creating a written goal, your odds of success increase a lot if you regularly check your progress and course correct as needed. I find this process to be rewarding in itself. Tracking your progress reinforces that *you can* do the various things you set out to do, thereby feeding your motivation to keep going and possibly working even harder towards each of your goals.

Life Hack #5: Aim high! As I look back on my career, one thing I've realized is my "VP by 33" goal was probably too low of a bar...or maybe I should have reset my career aspirations with a different goal once that original VP goal became a reality.

It's rare, in my experience, that you will ever overshoot a significant goal, so be careful you are not too conservative in establishing your goals. Reassess these from time to time to see if a bigger goal might be within your grasp. This is key to growing and reaching your full potential.

Professional goals

The above framework for goal setting, establishing tactics and monitoring progress, works equally well in your professional life, whatever career path you take. As I note in the next chapter on "Your Personal Inventory," the "Professional" inventory item would include goals and objectives you want to achieve in your career, but the goals and tactics approach described above also works well on specific projects and tasks you need to tackle at work. In my opinion, having a similar process and approach to implement in both your professional and personal life works really well together.

An acronym frequently used in human resource circles to help define a good goal is "SMART" which stands for Specific, Measurable, Achievable, Relevant, Time-based. I've found this SMART term is useful whether I am making a personal or professional goal. If the goal is not specific and measurable, it can be hard to tell if you've actually achieved the goal. If the goal is impossible and not achievable, you are likely setting yourself up for disappointment no matter how hard you try. If the goal is not relevant, what's the point of working towards it? The final time-based piece is also really important, this sets the deadline of when you commit to yourself you will complete the goal.

Even though they are each simple, one sentence goals, each of the five goal examples listed above meet the SMART criteria...goals don't have to be long and complicated to be SMART.

Family goal-setting and personal responsibility

Not to be too fixated on goal setting for every aspect of your life, but there is some real benefit in applying the tools and concepts described above with your family, if you have one.

There are big gaps in our public education system related to teaching goal-setting, personal responsibility, and money management skills, as well as providing more in-depth resources related to different career options in today's post-pandemic economy.

I believe it is important for kids, from a fairly early age, to understand they are responsible for themselves and not allow them to even start down the path of blaming others or, God-forbid, "society" for their problems and shortcomings. Instilling in kids the "you own you" mindset early, and teaching them that one of the positive ways they can improve their situation is by thinking through and developing simple goals and then following through on them. These simple goals can be sports or school related or as simple as learning a new hobby or skill. To the extent these can be tied into broader family activities, all the better.

It can also be really helpful to share with your kids the process you go through to address areas you are targeting for improvement in your life. It helps them understand that it's not always easy or automatic for mom and dad to magically make changes...it takes work, commitment, and sometimes course corrections to achieve all you want out of life.

The bottom line is that effective goal setting is a fundamental tool you can use to put yourself on a clear path to becoming the person you want to be in the future. Like any skill, the more you practice goal-setting and the activities that support working towards fulfillment of the goal, the better you will get utilizing this process. Give it a try!

Chapter 4

Your Personal Inventory

When I was young I was a worrier; from tornado warnings, to fear over a parent's illness, to my dog running away. I stressed in major ways as a kid and this progressively got worse as I entered my early teen years. It got to the point where, at times when I was 12 and 13, I would have trouble sleeping because I was worried about one thing or another.

In hindsight, I would say in today's terms, I was probably having some level of anxiety attacks. Sometimes these really frightened me and, for some reason, I never told anyone about these issues. At the time, I guess I thought people might think I was crazy.

As Nietzsche said, "that which does not kill us, makes us stronger," and truly out of these rough experiences I developed at an early age, what I now call "My Personal Inventory." Like a properly used Day-Timer, My Personal Inventory is a method I devised out of necessity, to help organize my thoughts, concerns, and priorities.

Like praying is for me, I found the best time to mentally go through My Personal Inventory was after going to bed, when I didn't have a lot of distractions. Again, like praying, another benefit of going though this while in bed was that it would usually relax me, allowing me to organize what was going on in my life, and to think about what I needed to focus on most the following day. This helped put me in a better frame of mind to sleep.

After getting in the habit of going through My Personal Inventory on a regular basis, I found I didn't need to worry about things nearly as much. It really helped me through those rough early teen years.

I've used this tool ever since and, while not so frequently, I still use this mental tool from time to time today, when my life seems to be unusually chaotic. As noted in the previous chapter, I also use the categories of My Personal Inventory when I reset my goals each year: the different categories serve as a handy reminder to make sure I am covering all the important elements of my life. Like setting goals, I think you will find, if you are not already doing your own form of a Personal Inventory, incorporating this tool into your regular thought routine may help reduce stress in your life, and help you better focus on those areas which really require your attention.

My Personal Inventory has evolved a bit as I have gotten older and it's changed some over the years. Here's the list I mentally go through periodically when I have time, or when I feel like life is starting to get out of control with too may pressing issues:

- Physically
- Mentally
- Spiritually
- Family
- Romantically
- Socially
- Financially
- Professionally
- Personally

This is the exact order I have had running through my head for most of my adult life. I'm not sure why the order is the way it is but, to some degree, it probably reflects how these categories have evolved since I began using My Personal Inventory in my teen years, with the later categories added as I got older.

Putting your Personal Inventory to use:

When I mentally go through each Personal Inventory category my focus is on, how am I doing in each of these parts of my life? Which of these do I want/need to prioritize, to improve, or conversely, am I focusing too much time on a given area? The reality is you can't be highly focused on all of these areas at the same time, so the value of going through the inventory is that it helps you prioritize the ones that need the most attention right now. It also helps you flag important areas of your life that you may be currently ignoring due to other pressing issues.

I have found using My Personal Inventory ***helps keep my life in balance***. I've stressed to my kids (though sometimes they don't listen!) the importance of keeping life in balance; that too much or too little of just about anything tends to not be good for you. As it relates to My Personal Inventory, it's easy for one or more of the items to be dominant, or perhaps I'm not focused at all on a given inventory item at certain stages of life. Going through the Personal Inventory helps you sanity check if your current prioritization is really optimal for you at that point in time, or if adjustments should be made; **Are you controlling your life, or is your life controlling you?**

For example, you might be really slammed at work (the "Professional" component of the inventory) where your attention needs to be highly focused in that one area for an extended period of time. Going through the inventory can sometimes flag the fact you've not been paying enough attention to your wife and kids given the work situation. Often, this can allow you to reflect and course correct on that element in your life, before your family situation gets severely impacted and, potentially, irreversibly damaged.

Here's an overview of how I think through each of the elements of My Personal Inventory:

Physically:

- I think through how am I from an overall wellness standpoint?

- If I have exercise or weight loss goals, am I on track with these?
- Do I need to exercise more? If so, what am I going to do about it (from here it might get loaded as a goal or tactic)?
- Do I need to lose weight (always one of my goals, and also one of my frustrations that I haven't gotten to where I want to be… yet!)?
- Do I need to schedule a physical, etc?
- Am I getting enough sleep?

Mentally:

- How am I feeling mentally?
- Is my stress level good?
- Am I interacting with kids, wife, coworkers, and others in a positive way?
- Is my energy level good?
- Am I happy?

Are there any specific actions I need to take to address concerns?

Spiritually:

- My faith is important to me. I couldn't imagine living a fulfilling, happy life without faith being at the center of it. At the same time, it's an element of my life that can easily be taken for granted. Thinking about faith as part of My Personal Inventory is really helpful to ensure I remain centered.
- Am I doing well on my personal spiritual objectives?
- Am I taking regular time during the week to pray and be thankful?

- How has my church attendance been?
- Have I been taking time to read the Bible?
- Have I been charitable?
- When our kids were still at home, I would think through how we were doing as stewards of our kids' faith journey.
- And the final, tough reality check: Am I living a Godly life?

Family:

- Like faith, I can't imagine living a truly happy, fulfilling life without my family. As noted, I've been blessed to have been married to my wife, Cathy, for 35 years, and have two really good and interesting, though very different, grown sons. I know many people don't have families and are happy not being married, and/or not having kids. For those folks, this part of their inventory might be better titled, "Relationships."
- For this part of the inventory I think about the quality of the relationships:
- With my kids?
- With my wife?
- With our parents?
- With our extended family?
- Am I in balance here and meeting my objectives in terms of:
- Spending quality time?
- Coaching, boating, camping or whatever other important family activities you want to prioritize…is that happening?
- Is my family time getting the proper allocation of my time relative

to work, or am I drifting to an out of balance condition?

Romantically:

- How's your love life? Depending where you are in life, this can either be your number one priority 24/7 or, perhaps later on in life, after being married for a while, it can sadly slip to the afterthought category. Regardless, hitting this topic on your Personal Inventory forces you to think about if you are happy romantically and, as importantly, how does your significant other feel?

- At the height of a busy career, or set of careers for each spouse, taking time for each other can be a challenge at times. Thinking and, ideally, talking about this from time to time, might serve as an early warning indicator that you need to allocate more time for each other, so you can continue building your relationship before it deteriorates.

- Are we really communicating openly and regularly?

- What can I do to make my significant other happier?

Socially:

- When we were raising our family, like many men I know with younger kids, I tended to allocate 100% my time to either my family or my job, and almost none to my social life. Most of the "friends" I had made since college had either been husbands of my wife's friends or fathers of my kid's friends. I enjoyed these relationships and the socialization they allowed.

- Given how much I had to travel in my career, and to allocate more time with my family, I gladly gave up golfing in a league and going out periodically with the guys. Time with my family was my priority for any free time and I have no regrets. Many people do regret this kind of tradeoff and it's an area that can cause significant conflicts if not thought through and addressed.

- Either way, the social part of your life is an important area to consider from time to time to see if it is meeting your needs.

- When your kids launch and you become an empty nester, this area often needs more focus. After years of perhaps not prioritizing this area, how do you now develop more social relationships? Many parents have a lot of anxiety as they enter their empty nester years, so it's worth allocating some time to think and talk about it with your spouse. This time can be a whole new exciting chapter in your lives, where you are much more free to have fun and develop new interests, but it takes some forethought to make the transition happily together with your spouse.

- If you decide to move somewhere else, think about what's the best way to ensure you have a good social life in the new location?

Financially:

- For me, investing has never really been focused on the acquisition of more material things. Like my parents, the accumulation of financial wealth has always been primarily focused on security for my family. Hitting this part of My Personal Inventory allows me to quickly calibrate how I'm doing and prioritize any changes that need to be made:

- Am I saving the right amount?

- Are we spending within our targeted budget?

- Am I investing our savings optimally?

- Is my investment portfolio where it should be, (more on these specific financial topics are covered in much more detail later in the book)?

- Are my charitable donations on track?

Professionally:

- This element focuses on sorting out the short term and longer term issues in your work life.
- If somehow you've derailed from the career path you want to follow, thinking about this inventory item will force you to think through and confront the issues and options to change course if needed:
- Are you happy where you work and what you do?
- If not, what are you going to do about it?
- Do you need to start a job search?
- Take additional training or courses?
- Ask your boss for a raise?
- In the post-pandemic era we are entering, you might be running your own business, or you might be developing multiple revenue streams in your slash career. These newer career paths make this thought process potentially more complex, but even more important because you don't simply have to just appease a boss to move up, you have to actually make it happen yourself in the real-world economy.
- Whether you are in a traditional career or making it on your own, if professionally, things are going well for you, do you need to recalibrate your goals and *set them higher?*
- How do you maximize your current good momentum and accelerate *faster?*

Personally:

- For me, this final category on the Personal Inventory, is kind of a "catch all" for anything that's not clearly covered in the previous inventory categories. It also provides an opportunity to ask the big question, "am I getting what I want out of life?"

- For example, my near term personal goals in this category are: all the tasks associated with getting this book published, learning some new songs on the guitar, and finding a boat to cruise America's Great Loop in the next year or two (America's Great Loop is the journey, traveling by boat, around the eastern part of North America).
- At some stages of your life, this category might be somewhat of an afterthought. At my current stage of life, each of these things are very high on my priority/importance list.

Your Personal Inventory should tie into and connect to your overall goals and tactics discussed in Chapter 3. If you are like me, the frequency with which you will review your Personal Inventory will most likely be based on the current stress level in your life. It could vary daily (as noted, before going to sleep) to maybe once every month or so if life is flowing beautifully.

Going through My Personal Inventory has always had a calming, centering effect on me. Like those who swear by a Day-Timer or some other similar tool, your Personal Inventory allows you to deal with the issues, successes, and areas for improvement at that point in time. From these, you can prioritize your future actions so you can move on to actually accomplishing these priorities. It helps keep your life from swinging out of balance.

Life Hack #6: What does your Personal Inventory look like?Consider developing your Personal Inventory and make the categories fit the most important areas of your life. You will find this particularly valuable if you are going through a time of big changes, or have a high level of stress and confusion in your life. My list has evolved and changed over time. For example, "School" was a big category on My Personal Inventory list until I completed grad school. Now it's not relevant, so I dropped it from the inventory list.

Chapter 5

The Big Career Choice: To College or Not to College?

"Yes there are two paths you can go by, but in the long run, there's still time to change the road you're on"-Stairway to Heaven-Led Zeppelin

When I was growing up, in my family at least, it was an absolute foregone conclusion that when you graduated from high school, you would go to college. At the time, at least in my family's world view, that was the best way to ensure a successful career and life.

My dad grew up in the depression extremely poor. He literally did not have indoor plumbing or central heat in the house he was raised in until he was 13 years old. After enlisting in the Navy after high school at age 17, and catching the tail end of World War II, the GI Bill provided his opportunity to be the first in his family to attend and graduate from college. For my dad, that college degree was his ticket to exit poverty, and so it is for many still today.

I raised both of my sons the way I was raised: "you will go to college no ifs, ands, or buts." What they chose to pursue in college was their choice, with input from me as needed, but whether or not they would go to college was not open for debate.

Good grades were also expected from both of my sons. They both developed excellent study habits, did well in school, and both were inducted into National Honor Society in high school. Once they got into junior high, we never had to chase either of them to do homework or to study. I am not sure this was the result of our parenting, or just having two really smart kids in a good public school system. They both had their choice of many colleges to pick from and received scholarship offers from several.

After the pandemic, the world has changed

Even as a kid my older son always enjoyed writing and creating stories. So we were not surprised that he wanted to pursue creative writing in college. He did so at Miami University, where he graduated with honors. He is now working, to me at least, the epitome of a slash career, which is generally defined as having multiple concurrent careers (hence a "/" sash between each one) all with a goal of achieving longer term career objectives. Becoming a successful novelist and/or screenplay writer, which is what my older son aspires to, is not a typical linear career path where you go work for someone and poof, you've got successful novels on the best seller list. It takes perseverance, skill, and certainly some luck.

So, while my son is now working on a second novel and various other screenplay writing projects, he is also doing freelance publicity and ghost writing. He also does free lance video production work and works for the city he lives in doing IT and communications work. All of these activities have a common thread of building skills, experiences, and contacts that will hopefully connect with his ultimate goal of being a successful published writer.

The beauty of the various slash jobs he has is that these still allow him time to focus on his craft. This likely would not be as easy if he were working in a more traditional, full time gig. My son's wife, who was a business major at Miami, and now works as a manager in supply chain and logistics, can support his efforts to get his much more high risk/potentially high reward writing career fully off the ground. They went into their marriage knowing this was the game plan, so it works for them.

The slash career is a prime example of the new wave of real career options that have been turbocharged during the pandemic.

My younger son provides a different example of new career options that got turbocharged during the pandemic: starting your own business. He developed a passion for music early in his teens. By the time he was 14, he started creating and marketing beats online. For those older readers like myself, “beats” are melodies to which lyrics can be added to create a complete song, which then can be marketed and licensed.

He taught himself a variety of instruments as well as various music production software programs required to produce the music. He then figured out various platforms where he could market his beats online. He read every book he could find on the music industry and music intellectual property so that he could navigate the fairly complicated field of music intellectual property. By doing so he was able to develop solid licensing agreements for his beats, all in his mid-teens.

Initially, when his beats weren’t selling well he invested about $1,000 in an online social media marketing course. It was offered by social media guru Tai Lopez. At this time my son was 15, and he spent about 100 hours over his Christmas break learning everything he could from the program. Following this course, his beats business took off. This business was his passion, and he focused all his waking energy on building it during the remainder of his high school years.

When it came time for college, there was still no debate (at least in my mind!) that he was going. The reality was, he could run his music business from anywhere. He selected Clemson’s business school and dual majored in accounting and finance. He also got involved in their entrepreneurial studies program.

In his freshman year he had a 3.9 grade average, while still trying to juggle his growing online music business. About half way through his freshman year, he made the decision that what he was learning at Clemson, he could easily learn on his own in a more time-efficient manner. Therefore, he believed the best plan would be to drop out of college after completing his freshman year, and focus his full energies on growing his music business. While that was hard for me to initially accept, his logic was sound and I knew his work ethic and passion would give him a decent opportunity to succeed.

After his Freshman year at Clemson, at the age of 19, he moved to Nashville. He used the money he earned from his beats business in high school to cover his living expenses. To his credit, he insisted on making it on his own with no help from mom and dad. Today, almost three years later, he is a successful music producer and artist manager who loves doing what he does for a living. While his first year or so was pretty lean from a financial standpoint, he is now earning far in excess of what he would have earned with a business degree coming out of Clemson at the age of 22.

I illustrate the above examples of my two sons because I think they're good representations of newer career options that exist for people today, and have been made even more relevant during the pandemic. College is still a great path for someone interested in a career that requires a college education. But, let's be honest, if the pandemic and the virtual learning Covid forced taught us anything, it's that paying 5-6 figures to learn in a college classroom is not the only way to learn valuable skills.

The reality is, there are strong forces that have brainwashed lots of folks (me included for many years), which state that everyone should go to college. The pandemic has shown, in many ways, that this is a fallacy. Many people go to college and get degrees in areas that have minimal value from a marketable employment standpoint. The bottom line is, there are no black and white, right or wrong answers, and while a college experience can be more than the job opportunities you have when you get your degree, it may not be the best option for everyone.

Trying to be as objective as I can be, the early success my younger son has achieved without a degree is fairly unique. He's always been driven and figured out early on what he wanted to do with his life. He went after it full throttle and has never let up. He's constantly learning, reading books, and listening to podcasts on a wide range of subjects.

Many younger folks may have a passing fancy with a job that seems like fun, but they may not actually be willing to put the time and effort in to get up the learning curve necessary to be a professional in that line of work. For young people who have frequently changing interests and passions, and/or don't know how to translate an interest into making a living out of it, the structure a college education provides can still be the best option.

Finally, don't forget the trades and all those valuable jobs that never required a four year college degree. In my view, public schools need to do a much better job earlier on in really explaining the options and trade offs of various career choices, and not simply focus on "90% of our high school graduates went on to college." Likewise, society and government could do everyone a favor by stopping the drumbeat of "free college" and "college is for everyone." It's not, and in a lot of cases, it's a total waste of the person's time as well as either that person's or society's money. Being a tradesperson such as a carpenter, pipe fitter, welder, etc., is highly valuable to our society. These jobs provide great careers with great pay, not only by working for someone else, but also by serving as a springboard to forming new businesses. To me, we should give people who choose these career options as much respect as anyone who goes to college.

Life Hack #7: Learn how to learn. I am sure we all knew kids who were straight-A students but they had minimal common sense. Moreover, they may have only done well in school when there was a course syllabus and a clear pathway marking out what was important to remember. Yet these same straight-A kids often struggle at actual life, where there is no defined syllabus.

We always told our kids that school grades were primarily important for allowing them the opportunity to pick the college they wanted to attend, that's how the system is set up. But we also stressed the importance of what they actually LEARNED, and more importantly, that they know where to go for resources to learn more about the subjects that interest them in the future.

This has been the key for my younger son. He came to the conclusion that he didn't need spoon-fed, college-guided learning. Instead, there is a world of learning opportunities for anything he needs for his business or personal development, all at his fingertips with the internet.

You can take control of your personal development, which can fuel your personal and professional growth by taking time to explore areas that interest you. It's as simple as using your smartphone for web searches, YouTube videos on just about anything, podcasts, and for those old-schoolers, there's the library.

To me, the smartest people figure this out early and crave new knowledge for its own sake. They are not trying to get a check mark in a book and a piece of paper affirming their knowledge. They are satisfying their never ending curiosity. Again, Learn how to Learn and you will be well ahead of the pack!

What's your passion?

When I started school at Ohio State, I knew I wanted to go into business. My first two years there I was convinced I wanted to be an accountant. I was always good at numbers, liked finance and investing, and my dad was a CPA, so I just kind of gravitated towards that part of the business program. Ultimately, after taking my first marketing class, along with 600 other souls in Lee Matthew's Principles of Marketing course, I discovered that marketing was my real interest, not accounting.

Early in that course, a summer business student exchange program at Ecole Superieure de Commerce de Nantes, in Nantes, France was offered as an option for those who wanted to apply. The program focused on all functional elements of commerce as it related to doing business in Europe, and all the classes were taught in English…a big key for me given I didn't speak French.

I applied for the program and was accepted. The experience was a life inflection point for me. Participating in the program, with a few dozen other American kids from a half dozen universities, opened my eyes to not only the bigger world, but also allowed me to understand how each of the business functions fit together. During this program I realized my passion was much better suited to a commercial profession rather than one in accounting.

I relay this story because while it is certainly a plus to have a good idea what you want to do for a career by the time you finish high school, it's important to have experiences. These experiences can occur either in your college years or early in your work life. They should allow you to understand what your initial career choice is really all about. For more traditional college bound kids, these experiences can include a study abroad, as in my case, or an internship or co-op which, thankfully, are much more common today than when I went to school.

For those kids going down one of the newer non-traditional paths of starting their own business, there is a wealth of resources available online. From actual remote learning courses to watching YouTubers explain how a particular thing is done or skill is learned. In my view, it's far better to get the career path right than to force yourself to complete a degree you know is not the right fit for you, just to complete your courses in four years (sorry moms and dads!).

Also, while finding a field of study you have some passion about is important, think through what types of actual jobs and career paths you potentially have when you complete that field of study. To the extent they provide this information at all, high schools and colleges generally do a poor job explaining the realities of what different degrees will really translate to in terms of future earning potential.

Here is a little clue: if you are looking at a field of study and the college advisor tells you that most of the co-ops and internships are unpaid for that field of study/degree, ask yourself why that is, and what does that portend for your future earnings potential?

As the parent helping their child sort through these choices, you have to ask yourself, is there a real value in what traditional college offers for the thing it is that your son or daughter wants to do in life? If your child wants to be a medical professional, engineer, or CPA, college is really the only path to take. For many other career choices, including sales, marketing, writing, music, and many other fields, the choice of going to college today is not as black and white as it was before the pandemic. There are many ways a person can try their hand and gain experience in these other types of career choices without signing up for a huge potential future debt load via the college route.

Reflecting upon the above changes in attitudes about college degrees, it's interesting to see that recently some large corporations are now offering internships and apprenticeships for non-college graduates as a way to onboard them into professional career paths that previously would have required a college degree. These companies, having gone through the pandemic and now having many holes to fill in their workforces, are implementing new, creative ways to keep their businesses properly staffed by growing their own talent.

At the same time, many parents and kids are waking up to the fact that spending six figures on a degree is not always a good investment in either time or money. This is especially evident as they have just spent a year or two still paying full tuition while their kids have been learning remotely, and perhaps realizing that much of that learning could have been had for free online.

As my kids grew up, the advice I gave them is to not worry so much about exactly what they want to do from a career standpoint, but to at least try to narrow it down to the type of career they want to pursue and what types of work really motivates them. While both of my kids figured out their passions at pretty early ages, many other kids struggle with figuring out what they want to do. For those that are grappling with this issue, I would encourage them to get some exposure to the areas they are interested in while still in high school, either through work, volunteering, or winging it by trying to create their own small business, either online or in the physical world.

Narrowing down to a general area of interest helps in another significant way, it saves time and money if you do elect to go down the traditional route of completing your college degree, assuming college is best suited to those interests. In my case, when going through this career thought process, marketing and accounting were both majors that were part of the college of business. Switching from one to the other mid way through my college career didn't really cost me much time in terms of earning my degree. All of the general course requirements and most of the basic business requirements I took in my first two years fully applied to both marketing and accounting, so I was still able to graduate within four years. If you begin college wanting to be a doctor and then switch in year four to wanting to be a mechanical engineer, the impact on time and cost to complete your degree will likely be a lot greater.

As a parent you can also help by providing input from your observations of your child's interests while they are growing up. My parents pretty much let me find my own way in terms of choosing a major. But in hindsight, from the time I was in grade school, I was always selling something, from selling gum in grade school in order to save enough money to buy a phone for my room, to making and selling chocolate bunnies in junior high to make extra money. An objective observer would say I was destined for a career in sales. However, this never dawned on me until I was working in marketing for several years and gradually gravitated to sales and ultimately, sales management.

What's your dream career?

Whether you are in high school, college, or even in the workforce, it might be helpful to step back and look at what interests you. For example, what kinds of jobs and activities you gravitated towards while growing up, what you like to do versus what you don't like to do, then compare these insights versus what you are planning to do for a career. I think many times people find they are pursuing a career path for the wrong reasons: money, it's what their parents do for a living, it's what everyone expects them to do, it seems exciting, etc.

And consider all options before signing that first tuition check!

The decades-long societal mantra that college is best for everyone is crazy. There are excellent opportunities and high demand for skilled tradespeople, and a very good lifestyle is possible in these careers. There are also never-before-seen opportunities to launch your own business using technology, if you are so inclined. Resources are widely available to learn just about anything, much of it for free, on the internet, through podcasts, and other sources. The real challenge for you to consider is; are you motivated and do you have the perseverance to make this happen?

Coming out of the pandemic, I'd be seriously evaluating my value position if I were a college president. For many years, most colleges have relied on almost unlimited public funding as they, along with other societal "thought leaders," convinced huge swathes of the population that the only way to be a "successful" person is to have a college degree.

In most cases, colleges aren't being challenged to justify the return on investment (ROI) to either the students, parents, or, for that matter, the taxpayers who are footing the bill. If I am a person who worked their tail off right out of high school building my own business, why on earth would I feel it's now my responsibility to pay for the college tuition of someone who took out a bunch of student loans and now can't pay them back? In many cases, this is due to the fact the degree they earned is worthless from an earnings standpoint. Ultimately, the public money gravy train will have to stop and colleges will have to find ways to provide an ROI for the investment people make in attending because now there are too many competing options out there for prospective students to consider.

You have more power as an employee

From an employer standpoint, the pandemic has really altered the axis of power in their relationships with their employees. As of February, 2022, according to the U.S. Bureau of Labor Statistics, there are 10.9 million job openings but only 6.3 million unemployed people looking for jobs.

In addition, the "Great Resignation" has resulted in an unprecedented number of people, including about 90% who are 55 years old or older, who have decided they no longer want to work, at least in the way they have in the past (I'm living proof of that!). In November, 2021 for example, 3.6 million more people left the labor force with no intention of returning compared to November, 2019 before the pandemic according to Aaron Sojourner, a labor economist and professor at the University of Minnesota.

The reality is, millions of people, having come through the pandemic, have reassessed their priorities, often deciding what they have been doing for work is not the same priority it was before the pandemic.

When there are almost twice as many available jobs as job seekers, and you figure in that millions of highly experienced, more senior workers have exited the workforce for good, the job seekers and workers that remain have a lot more options and therefore, power.

This is a pretty seismic change; companies can no longer assume there will be flocks of people waiting in line to apply for every available job that is posted. Employers will have to compete hard just to find bodies to fill roles and to retain long term loyal employees. They will have to continually address and increase pay levels and provide more creative solutions like offering apprenticeship programs for non-college graduates. To retain loyal employees, employers may have to once again consider offering company pensions. I believe we may be entering a golden age for workers, where the options and opportunities are far greater than they have been in our lifetimes.

Life Hack #8: The sooner you realize what truly interests you and what possible careers fit with these interests, the more likely you will find a career that fits you well for the long term and where you can excel. In today's economy, the sky is the limit for what an individual can do, often without need for a college degree if you are sufficiently motived and willing to learn and work on your own to achieve your goals.

The same holds for those struggling in a dead-end job or career. There has never been a better time to take a chance on doing something different that you are passionate about. Chances are, if it doesn't work out, your old job will likely still be there waiting for you!

It's a cliché but true: we spend at least 1/3 of our lives working. It is well worth the effort to take the time for serious thought on what truly fits your personal interests to help ensure a happy, fulfilling life. One of the many beautiful things of working in a still largely free country like the USA is that no matter what stage you are at in life, it's never too late to change course and do something different!

Chapter 6

What Are Your Goals For Your First Job?

After you have completed your formal education or opted to enter the workforce without college, you are now primed for your first full-time gig. This is an exciting and challenging time and an important period to take stock as you start building your career and launching your adult life. Paths established in the first few years in the work force affect your trajectory in life such as what career path you will take, where you will live, if and when you will start a family, and if and how you will prepare for major investments (house, retirement, etc.) for the future.

I have worked with many Millennials and Gen Z'ers and have observed my two sons' experiences as they've launched their somewhat non-traditional careers. One of the things that motivated me to sit down and finish this book was seeing the opportunities and challenges that confront young people as they enter the workplace today. With the recent pandemic, things have changed even more dramatically as it relates to what "work" means and how it is now conducted by both new people entering the workforce and those already established in their careers.

In my view, there are three significant changes affecting people entering the workforce today that did not impact me when I started out:

1. First, people today grew up in a time where part-time jobs, for the most part, were plentiful during their high school and college years. When I grew up, even a job in fast food in high school was prized. People today have grown up with the knowledge that if they became bored, or did not like their boss at Arby's or the

Gap, they could simply quit and walk down the street to get a new job. Employers have generally needed entry level workers more than the workers desperately needed a job. That trend has now been dramatically heightened with the pandemic. It seems like virtually everyone is hiring for almost every type of role, from entry level to management. For entry level roles, it's almost become the norm that employers are offering a pay that is far above the legal minimum wage, often with signing bonuses and other perks. This is an element of the axis shift between labor and employers I noted earlier.

2. The second intertwined factor, and this ties into a broader societal focus for kids to have "positive self-esteem," is that parents today often seem to try to become their kid's best friend, rather than a role model (believe me, I fought this urge with my own kids). Parents are much more highly involved in their kids' lives while growing up and through the college years than when I was young. I think, at least in part, this is due to wanting to ensure their kid's safety. Additionally, I believe parents often fear their kids growing up and leaving the nest, so they end up micromanaging details of their kids' lives through college and beyond. In my view, this delays the kids having to deal with many of the realities of life, including stumbling and making mistakes that are critical for future growth. Rather than helping, parents may actually be stunting their kid's development.

3. The third change had already begun but the pandemic kicked it into overdrive. The gig economy has given rise to several newer modes of working. These include the choice to launch a business (many of these being online in nature), the choice to not be a "wage slave," as my younger son would say, and the aforementioned "slash" career option. Regardless of how or where you work, you are likely doing it more remotely now than you ever dreamed possible. For those established in traditional careers, this long term ability to work remotely has opened

opportunities to live in more interesting and/or less expensive places. It also provides the opportunity to moonlight and develop other revenue streams. I wouldn't define it as a slash career; it's more like a main career with another significant side job, which can dramatically increase your earnings potential.

Taken together, these changes have resulted in younger workers having dramatically different expectations of what work means, and their employers must understand that they need to be more flexible and accommodating to hire, motivate, and retain these younger workers. The added freedom that expanded remote work creates makes the loyalty bond between worker and employer even more tenuous. These factors have washed over to people already established in their careers, including dinosaurs like myself. I admire and agree with the attitude that has evolved in recent years in which workers should not view themselves as beholden to an employer who doesn't strive to properly motivate, compensate, and value the employee.

A recent survey noted that at the beginning of 2021, larger businesses anticipated that 10-15% of their workforce, who had been working remotely due to the pandemic, would not agree to returning to work in an office after Covid work restrictions were lifted. A year later, employers are finding that actually 55-60% of workers at all stages of their careers are essentially saying, "take this job and shove it" if you demand I return to work out of an office.

I find it interesting that mega companies, like Facebook and Google, keep pushing back their "return to the office" dates due to "the ongoing pandemic." The reality is they know they've lost control of the situation and can't afford to lose half of their workforce by mandating office work. After the pandemic, I think virtually all companies will find it difficult to get the "monkeys" to go back to working from their "cages," er cubes, 40 hours a week. This goes for older workers just as much as younger workers. This trend is already starting to have profound ramifications for office space needs as well as real estate values in many parts of the country....just try to buy a house or condo in Florida!

The effects of these changes have been somewhat revolutionary in many aspects of the traditional employee/employer relationship in the Americas. Long gone is almost any expectation, on either side of the table, that when a worker starts with a new employer they will remain with that employer most, let alone all, of their career.

In many cases, there has been a real power shift from the employer to the worker, especially coming out of the pandemic. I don't think this has been fully realized by most employers even today. New employees not only expect to be paid fairly, but they also expect opportunities to be proactively offered for them to grow with the business quickly, within months or a year or two. They don't want to wait 5-10 years for growth opportunities. Workers also expect their employer to engage them from a social perspective, to be environmentally conscious and, to some extent, to be "woke" socially and politically.

These employees are also much more focused on work life balance and will more often than not, always be on the look-out for better opportunities. Many will have side gigs and be interested or already exploring entrepreneurial opportunities while working. They will absolutely need flexibility in hours as well as where and how they work.

How can you take advantage of these exciting changes?

The focus of this book is on how you can achieve *your* full potential. On the heels of the pandemic, the reality is many, if not most, employers are playing catch up with these trends and trying to determine how they will pivot to operate optimally in the future. As you navigate the workplace, it's important for you to factor in some of these old, somewhat outdated employer views.

For employers, to the nimble go the spoils in terms of capturing the best, most engaged and durable workforce. Make no mistake, while presenting a different and more challenging proposition in terms of management and retention, these younger workers often have innovative and valuable ideas, which can help the businesses they work for grow their profits.

Life Hack #9: Throughout your life, but particularly as you grow in your career, the most critical skill to ensure you are getting all you deserve, both in and out of the workforce, is being able to negotiate effectively. In order to negotiate well, your ability to empathize and have good listening skills are absolutely essential.

Empathy means putting yourself in the other person's shoes and seeing the world from their perspective. Not necessarily because you agree with whatever they want to do, but because it's hard to find negotiating angles if you don't understand their world view and what motivates them.

In a negotiation, to be able to empathize, you first need to shut your trap and listen! When you do talk, you are first trying to ascertain what makes the person you are talking to tick in an honest, non-patronizing way. Empathizing is true for both your professional life as well as your personal life. Whether you are interviewing for a new job, trying to make a sale, working with a new boss, negotiating to buy a house, or working through any other type of negotiation in your personal life such as with your wife, kids, neighbors, etc. the ability to empathize is key. I have noted a few excellent books on the art of negotiation in the selected reference section at the back of the book.

Life Hack #10: Empathy is critical in your professional life. Before making critical career choices such as your response to a proposed change in work structure, a

promotion, a requested lateral move, or a request for you to relocate, take time for some careful consideration and avoid an immediate reaction. Try to anticipate how your boss, mentor, and other senior managers in the organization will react to your decision and how this reaction could impact your future trajectory within the company. Consider if your manager or others would lose face by your decision. Your decision may be completely rationale to you, but it can still adversely impact your future potential advancement within an organization, so it's important you are conscious of that potential...choose your battles wisely!

Here's where I will provide a dual track for my advice: one track for the younger person entering or still new in their career, and one track for those who are established in their careers:

Millennials and Gen Z'ers

Perhaps because they are somewhat new to the work world, or maybe because just about everyone for their entire lives has been bending over backwards to make sure their self-esteem is in tact, my observation is Millennials and Gen Z'ers are generally pretty bad at the whole empathy thing, they are often very self-absorbed (sorry if that hurts your feelings!). Despite their "woke" sensibilities, they frequently do not go out of their way to try to "live in the other person's skin" much. As a result, they can really shoot themselves in the foot when encountering an older, battle hardened boss or other key influencer in their work environment.

Here's a real example from my past work. I, along with one of my colleagues, was interviewing a candidate in their late 20's. This person was in our management development program and being considered for a potential promotion to a Key Account Management role. The promotion would mean a higher base salary, bigger bonus potential, and greater responsibility managing one of the business's most important customer relationships.

Rather than focusing primarily on what the role entailed and what the candidate needed to do in order to be successful, this person focused a significant part of the discussion on how quickly they would be considered for their *next* promotion. From mine and my colleague's perspectives, this was not only "putting the cart before the horse," but also it was borderline rude and very presumptuous for the candidate to think an automatic promotion was guaranteed to follow.

I'm generally a very straightforward person, so I told the candidate the best thing they could do to ensure any future potential promotion opportunities was to execute and deliver superior results as quickly as possible in the role being discussed. This seemed to stun them a bit; that another promotion was not a given, but was based on how this person actually performed! I fear this reaction is a little bit of the outcome of what I will call the "don't I get a trophy just for showing up even though I suck" attitude that has been nurtured by our society over the past few decades. This practice tries to make sure everyone feels they are an equal winner at whatever they attempt. Unfortunately for these delicate souls, at some point, the real world is likely to smack them upside the head. The quicker you learn that in the vast majority of cases, you and the results you produce control the trajectory of your career, the better.

Oldsters (those over 35!)

If you are in this demographic, you are well aware that not everything in work life is "candy canes and unicorns." Nothing is guaranteed and you know that you oftentimes earn what you get by effectively marketing yourself, listening for when opportunities arise, and negotiating for an outcome that meets your career aspirations.

It is really important at all stages of your career, that you don't get pigeon holed into a perceived limited area of expertise, you need to stay a vibrant learning creature. As I noted in Chapter 5, while I stressed a focus on achieving good grades with both of my sons as they were growing up, (because to some degree that is how colleges score success in the short term), I also always tried to focus them on the fact that what they *were actually learning* is what matters in the real world, not what their grades are or were: **You need to learn how to learn...that is most important.**

Today, expanding your knowledge is as easy as pulling out your smartphone:

- You can Duck Duck Go a topic related to your work, your industry, your future career aspirations, or any other topics that appeal to you. If you find a topic that's of interest, bookmark it so it's easy to return to.

- If you find an interesting channel or "YouTuber" on YouTube, subscribe to it. By doing so you will automatically get a notification any time that person or channel uploads new content (for the oldsters, there is no charge for subscribing to a YouTube channel!).

- Listen to a podcast on just about any topic you can think of. Your phone likely has a podcast app or you can listen to many interesting podcasters on Spotify.

Be a Learning Creature to achieve your full potential!

It's shocking to me how many adults I know, including good friends, both in and out of work, who have never read a book of any type, either for knowledge or for pure entertainment. Many in my age bracket also don't listen to podcasts or attempt to expand their knowledge in any other discernible way. In our warp-speed changing economy, you risk becoming obsolete quickly. Plus, to me, it seems like such a dull existence. Reading a recent Steven King novel for pleasure, the main character in the story was explaining how they preferred friends and acquaintances who read books to those who don't read: "they are just more interesting from a conversation standpoint once the conversation goes beyond today's weather." I couldn't agree more.

Listening

While some of the attitudes of the younger generations, as noted above, might drive you crazy if you've been around a while, it's worth trying to listen and understand where these folks are coming from. The reality is both older and younger folks can derive a lot of value by understanding each other's perspectives, but that only happens if people can listen and empathize.

For me, a recent example of this relates to cryptocurrencies. The vast majority of adults I know still view these assets as some sort of scam or ponzi scheme. I've heard many say, "If there is no such thing as an actual physical Bitcoin, how can it be worth anything?" My younger son, who consumes knowledge in all forms, almost like a machine, started sharing a number of articles and podcasts with me on what crypto is, and what different aspects of blockchain technology can do from a business transaction standpoint. Had I not been open minded enough to be willing to listen, I would have never learned how truly transformative cryptos and their underlying blockchain technology are likely to become. I'd have built a wall around the possibility of my learning about this subject, and likely lost an opportunity to develop yet another interesting connection point with my son. In fact, I believe cryptos will be so transformational that I've invested a lot of time over the past year learning all I can about them. In Chapter 16 I have included a distilled down version of this information that will hopefully spark your interest and shorten your learning curve.

Whether it be with a family member or a co-worker, the point is you need to be open to learning. You need to listen for the opportunities to learn from someone outside your age group and/or your normal social circle. You also need to be open to listening to different perspectives. As a result, you will learn and grow yourself.

What new opportunities can you pursue?

The dramatic changes in the employee/employer relationship and the emerging new ways of working described above will likely continue to be really important features of your career landscape for many years to come. The potential exists for much more freedom in creating your own work environment, whether that be a mix of revenue streams or the more traditional working arrangement with one employer. It's quite likely the norm of working in an office 40 hours per week for many Americans has changed for good. Embrace that change and think through the opportunities these changes can create for you.

Parents may need to adapt as well

For parents raising kids in high school and even college, it's a brave new world for you also. There are different gravitational pulls on kids today, some good and some not so good. For many kids, the traditional path of getting a degree or going into a trade is still by far the best option.

However, for kids that find their passion early and are driven to work hard to pursue that passion (not just dream about how cool it would be to be a YouTuber, for example, without actually doing the work and learning what it takes), there have never been fewer barriers to starting a business on their own. Parents must be open to switching gears and determining how they can support exploration of that path.

For me, raised as I was with the belief that college was the golden ticket for anyone who can afford it to help ensure a financially secure life, I won't lie, the concept of my younger son dropping out of college with a +3.9 GPA to pursue his music business full time took some getting used to. At the end of the day, the reason I supported my son's decision was that I had seen first hand the passion, work effort, and growth he had achieved in building his business while in high school. He wasn't just a talker and a dreamer. He was a doer who was willing to put in whatever effort was necessary to learn and grow his business. His every waking hour was consumed with doing the business or reading books and listening to podcasts about building his business. He had truly mastered the key concept of "learning how to learn." So, after some soul searching on what would be the right thing to do, I jumped in with both feet to offer any support I could.

The point of detailing this brief history is that the idea of building your own business is an attractive dream to almost everyone. And while the barriers to entry, in many ways, are lower than they have ever been, it still takes real hard work and fortitude, even in today's gig economy, to actually make a living doing it. For parents trying their best to support their kids through these types of choices, it can be a real challenge. Only you can judge if your child has what it takes to have a real chance at success. If they flit from one passing interest to another frequently and get frustrated when they don't have immediate success, it might be best to encourage them to stay the course in college or a trade. If the passion is real, they can still pursue their dream moonlighting while taking classes and perhaps make a change once they've actually started generating results with their business idea.

"Nothing in this world can take the place of persistence. Talent will not: nothing is more common than unsuccessful men with talent. Genius will not; unrewarded genius is almost a proverb. Education will not: the world is full of educated derelicts. Persistence and determination alone are omnipotent." President Calvin Coolidge

Life Hack #11: In my opinion, Calvin hits the nail right on the head: Perseverance and persistence are almost always the difference makers between success and failure. All jobs have their pros and cons! There is no such thing as a "perfect" job...even if you are trying to create your own job by building a business. You have to learn to persevere through issues you encounter that you don't like in a job. Like all setbacks and challenges in life, many times these are learning opportunities and you come out of these challenges a better, stronger, and more successful person.

There's still time to change the road you're on,

Landing on the right career path out of high school or college can be a challenging time for most people. The reality today is that few people actually end up staying at their first job for more than a year or two. For example, a recent US Bureau of Labor Statistics survey found that more than 55% of recent college graduates leave their employer within the first year of employment.

Many find out that their degree does not actually allow them to enter into their desired field. More frequently, new graduates find that they can get a position with a company that has a path to their chosen field, but it may take a few years to actually work their way into such a position. While I would not advocate sticking with your first job through thick and thin forever, you need to balance what you are looking for in terms of a career with a realistic assessment of your short and long term career expectations.

Sometimes, as in my own personal case, I found upon graduating with my BSBA in marketing, that to really get a job in "marketing" (ie product management, advertising, PR, market research, etc.), as opposed to selling, required an MBA. After a few attempts at different jobs after graduation, I took my GMAT, and entered into the full time MBA program at Case Western Reserve University the following winter semester. Not only was the program excellent, but it also helped facilitate an internship in market research with a company I later joined full time after graduation. Ultimately, I became their Vice President of Sales & Marketing.

After the excitement of landing a job offer, ask questions

When you consider accepting a given job, make sure you clearly understand the requirements (work hours, need to relocate, career path, how success will be judged, etc.). This is especially important today with so many of the traditional rules in flux. Don't ever be dazzled by a fancy job title (a frequent trick foisted on college grads is to throw "manager" into the title) or, God forbid, the "opportunity to travel." In each job, you need to use the skills and disciplines noted above. You should also write out your goals and tactics for the job. These tactics will help keep you moving down the path towards your longer term goals. At the same time, keeping your "bigger picture" long term goals in mind will help you navigate some of the short term unpleasant aspects of the assignment you are in now.

Life Hack #12 When you are going to high school, it is helpful to get a job that does not detract from your grades. If you have a demanding but fair boss, count yourself as lucky...this can be an excellent learning experience and can help you develop work ethic habits that can help set you apart later in your career.

Life Hack #13: If you go to college, try to focus on what really interests you and inspires passion, but also determine the real potential careers that connect with those interests so you understand the career and income potential from that choice. Then, work hard with professors and your placement department to get real-world work experience while still in school as early as possible in that field...even if the pay is poor. This will serve to help solidify your career choice and also provide helpful contacts and references for your job search prior to graduation...this experience can be far more valuable (even if it does not seem like it at the time) than the money you are actually paid.

Life Hack #14: Be careful you don't outgrow the pond you are swimming in! It can be really beneficial to join a smaller company, either right out of school or early in your career. The benefits can include having more responsibility than you might at a larger company as well as gaining exposure to how all the pieces of the business fit together.

That being said, if you are successful at climbing the ladder, you will likely find, at some point, you've outgrown that business. By staying longer, there is a good chance you will be placing a ceiling on your growth and earnings potential.

Chapter 7

Is Stress an Issue for You?

"Every time I thought I'd got it made, it seemed the taste was not so sweet"-Changes-David Bowie

As I noted at the start of chapter 4, I was a big worrier when I was a kid and, thankfully, I discovered my own Personal Inventory at a young age to help identify, prioritize, and deal with those worries in an organized, rationale way. In doing so, those worries became manageable: I managed the worry instead of the worry managing me.

Early in my married life, I hit another "wall of worry" that really affected and stressed me. After getting married and living in an apartment for about a year, my wife and I, both newly minted professional "yuppies," decided to buy our first house. We found a great French Tudor built in the 1930s in a revitalized part of West Akron, Ohio. The all brick house needed some work, but was a lot of house for the money, with classic features like copper spouting and a slate roof on an oak lined street…all for under $85,000! We found a local savings & loan for the mortgage and obtained a five year variable loan for 8.75%. I realize this mortgage rate seems obscenely high now, but this was in the late 80's, on the heels of Jimmy Carter's stagflation economy, when no one thought interest rates would ever be under 10% again. I hope, as I sit here in early 2022, we are not going down the Jimmy Carter path of out of control inflation once again!

Upon signing the mortgage with my wife, for the first time since my adolescence, I started having major anxiety. I worried, "what if I get fired or disabled and can't make the mortgage payments, what will become of our dreams?" I suppose, to one degree or another, everyone who signs their first mortgage and stares down the barrel of 30 years of debt goes through this stress. For me, it was major and almost out of control, even if somewhat irrational. While thinking through My Personal Inventory during this time helped, I was still absorbed by the impact of this new debt, worrying about where I would get the money to pay it off if something happened to me or my wife. This worry and stress literally consumed me for weeks. As usual, I really didn't confide what I was going through with anyone. Still pretty new to being married, I didn't want my wife to think I was crazy for stressing on this issue so much.

Luckily, during this time, I attended a work-related time management seminar that provided a very useful insight. While the name of the speaker and most of the content of the training session is lost to my memory, one piece of advice stuck with me and has served me well over the years. Like My Personal Inventory, it's a simple but powerful concept that, when applied consistently in your life, may simplify it and make it much less stressful.

The speaker at the conference was talking about how much time people spend worrying about issues in their lives that relate to money and other "trivial" matters when, in fact, if you asked people at the end of their lives what was most important, few would ever refer to anything that related to money. His point can be summarized as the following:

Life Hack #15: If an issue can be fixed by writing a check (meaning it can be solved with money), it is not a *problem*, it is an *expense*. Problems can merit worry, expenses don't.

On the surface, this may seem like semantics, but underneath is a powerful lesson. This statement hit home with me because it was directly applicable to my obsessive anxiety I was going through at the time. This new expense, my mortgage, was consuming my thoughts. When I applied this philosophy…to simply consider the mortgage an expense and not a real "problem"... it was like magic for me. All of a sudden, the worry went away. There are a hundred ways I can deal with an expense. For example, I could buy disability insurance if I was afraid of becoming disabled. I could take on a second job if I wanted to build more savings to buffer a potential job loss. I could look for a better paying job to make the mortgage payment a smaller portion of our income, etc. The point is, I could attack an expense in a variety of objective, non-emotional ways. An expense is a less personal issue to deal with than a true problem. It's like a fly landing on your arm at a picnic, you could stress about the fly, but most likely you will simply swat it away and get on with finishing your ham sandwich. The time I was investing in worrying about the mortgage and the "ifs and buts" of what if I couldn't make the payments down the road was a total waste of time. Far more productive was actively focusing on addressing the expense.

This approach has helped me many, many times in my life and continues to do so today. It's certainly helped me to be a more disciplined investor. Equity markets fluctuate but data for the past century shows that over the long run, US stocks as a whole go up. So, I don't stress and worry every time the market corrects. Instead, I evaluate the economic situation surrounding the decline and, most of the time, I end up buying into that decline rather than worrying and selling out of fear.

Rarely have my wife and I ever fought about money or financial issues (as you likely know, financial problems are the leading cause of divorce in the US). We attack these issues as expenses not as "problems." If the car transmission goes bad, we have a rationale discussion about whether we have the cash and what tradeoffs we have to make to cover the cost. There is no value in feeling bad about the transmission going bad...what's done is done. You can either get the car fixed (and perhaps factor this issue into the next brand of car you purchase), or you can start taking the bus or Uber when transportation is needed.

I bet every one who reads this book knows several people who spend a large part of their lives stressing about issues that money can solve. I have both family members and good friends who cannot enjoy a nice meal out or fully enjoy a family vacation without being somewhat consumed throughout the experience with the cost of each expenditure. They worry about how much money they are spending and, to some extent, feel bad that they are spending too much on this activity. Anyone who is descended from parents of the depression era has high odds of growing up with this approach to life.

When you step back and look at this, isn't it sad? How many vacations do we get to enjoy with our families? One or two each year if we're fortunate? Why waste these precious moments in your family's life with one second of worry about the cost? Don't get me wrong, I'm absolutely not advocating free spending and "damn the consequences." Far from it. What I am saying is treat your financial issues like a business, the "You Incorporated" business. Over the next chapters, I will talk about these financial issues in more detail, to hopefully help you get a grip on the money matters in your life. Try applying this concept of distinguishing between problems and expenses and it may help you live a happier life!

Life Hack #16: Don't waste a single moment of your precious life investing time in stress, worry, and anxiety into issues that are really expenses and can be fixed by writing a check. Deal with the expense and move on. Focus your concerns on those truly important things that money can't fix such as you and your family's health and happiness. I guarantee, you will live a richer life.

My Mantra:

In addition to the insight of separating actual problems from those that can be solved by writing a check, another really important tool that helped me during this anxious time was something I call My Mantra. I found this internal mantra served as a kind of simple diagnostic and really helped me settle down and focus on those things that mattered. It helped keep me on the right track when life was getting a little too out of balance.

I'm not sure how the specific elements of My Mantra developed. All I know is that since my late 20's, I've used the same set of components, in the order noted below, to think about when life gets a bit out of control and/or I am feeling down. I've found when that is happening, usually applying heightened focus on one of more of the areas in My Mantra helps get me back on track towards sustained happiness.

My Mantra is:

- Focus on the positive
- Live in the middle
- Help other people
- Do the right thing

Focus on the positive: It seems the world is filled with many negative people and ideas as well as many forms of "entertainment" that can seep into our core being over time like a toxin. At a certain point, all this negative energy and intent can start affecting our outlook and level of happiness. So, it seems pretty logical that when I am getting frazzled or feeling down, focusing on the positive would help, but what this also means is *actively avoiding the negative.* That can mean avoiding negative people in our lives, stop watching the news, and/or stopping your consumption of music, video games, or movies with negative or evil/violent themes (which can greatly limit your options on Netflix!). When you focus on the positive, you come to appreciate how much corrosive negative energy (and I would say in a lot of cases, real evil) is out there in the world that can be avoided.

Live in the middle: This goes back to the concept of balance discussed earlier. In this element of the mantra, I'm thinking about:

- How is my sleep…am I getting too little or too much?
- Am I eating right or have I been eating a lot of junk or fast food?
- Am I working too many hours?
- Have I been out partying too much?
- Have I been getting the right amount of exercise?

Usually, when I am feeling like life is getting out of control, it's because one or more elements of my daily life are not properly balanced.

Help other people: This isn't just a do-gooder concept. I was fortunate to learn at an early age that helping others, in an ironically selfish kind of way, made me feel really good about myself.

Again, when my life is a bit out of whack and/or I am feeling down, a lot of times, upon reflection, I will note I've been pretty self-absorbed in the recent past, and only focused on "me." When I notice this, I force myself to think of some ways I can do something for others. It can be as simple as making a phone call to someone who might be lonely or would appreciate the call. It could be shoveling the neighbor's sidewalk without them even knowing it. It could be skipping a guy's night out and taking the kids camping, or to a ballgame. The point is, putting the focus on someone else and away from yourself and, by doing so, actually making you feel better about yourself. The benefits flow to the giver as much as to the receiver.

Do the Right Thing: Again, this can sound corny, but I've found at times when I am not quite centered and hitting on all cylinders, upon reflection, I will sometimes find I am not doing everything in my life to the standard I should be.

This doesn't have to be major law breaking, it can be as simple as not giving 100% in your relationships, not being as generous as you might be with your church or favorite charity, or maybe you are not being as honest as you should be in certain situations in your life.

To me, this is your conscience subtlety telling you "Hey! Fix this!" before the issue manifests itself in some bigger way.

The specific components of My Mantra might not be exactly right for you. It's important to note that while My Mantra can certainly be viewed as being focused on living a virtuous life to some extent, it evolved for purely selfish reasons: to help me be more consistently happy, which is always my ultimate goal.

I have found in my life, as the saying goes, virtue is its own reward and that if you intentionally seek the positive, try to live in balance doing the right thing and helping other people, you will attain a higher level of happiness on a sustained basis. That's way more valuable, at least to me, than the number of zeros you have on a piece of paper from your broker.

Life Hack #17: See if there is a personal mantra that would help you. Like the Personal Inventory, going through the mantra after going to bed, when the world around you is quiet, is a great time to sort things out and recalibrate. For those spiritually minded, doing this after praying certainly doesn't hurt the process of having the right order of things in your life fall into place.

Knock on wood, but since developing and utilizing My Personal Inventory and My Mantra, I've not had any significant anxiety since the mortgage stress in my 20's and I've been phenomenally happy. The fact is: *you control you*, and if negative thoughts start rattling around in your head, hard as it may seem at the time, <u>you have the power to shut them down quickly.</u> Once you know this and exert control over your thoughts, you will find it miraculous how fast your life can return to normal. <u>You own you and you control you...believe it!</u>

Chapter 8

Recognizing Career Inflection Points

What's an inflection point? I use this term to indicate a major crossroad in your life. Earlier in the book, I related the story of how I quit smoking. I hit a crossroads decision after I mistakenly bought a pack of smokes the morning after I intended to quit. That crossroads, or inflection point, in my life was clear to me as many personal inflection points are; you are confronted with a clear choice: do I throw the pack away and start my life a a non-smoker, or do I keep on smoking?

Career inflection points, while maybe not the life and death choice that choosing to quit smoking is, can have a significant impact on your life nonetheless. In addition, career inflection points are frequently not as obvious as those crossroads decisions we encounter in our personal lives. When I think back on my career, and in particular, how I achieved my first big career goal of becoming a "VP by 33," a part of that was acting on an inflection point I recognized at that point in my career.

This chapter is primarily aimed at those working in an organization with aspirations of climbing the ladder to a higher level with more money and responsibility. That said, the points made in this chapter can also be useful in positioning yourself for greater success no matter what you choose to do in life.

The somewhat boring truth is most of your career involves mostly showing up and performing at or above the expectations of what you are paid to do. Real life-changing opportunities, or inflection points, come along very infrequently. However, there will be a handful of times where you come upon an inflection point that can dramatically change the trajectory of your career and, more broadly, your life. Typically, no one tells you what these inflection points are, or when they will occur…it's up to you to recognize and capitalize on them to maximize your career trajectory.

I will start by giving an example from my own career whereupon I recognized an inflection point when it arose and took action to move my career in a whole new direction…this is the inflection point that was key for me achieving my "VP by 33" goal.

When I was working on my MBA at Case Western Reserve in Cleveland, I did a summer internship with a company whose owner, Al Weatherhead, was the benefactor of the Weatherhead School of Management at Case. Upon graduating, I was offered a position as this company's first marketing manager and, a few years later, at the advice of the company's president at the time, I accepted a lateral sales role to get more direct experience with customers.

There came a time in my early 30's when that president was promoted to run one of Al Weatherhead's other businesses and my boss at the time, who was the VP of Sales & Marketing, was promoted into the president's role. This left a vacancy for the role of VP of Sales and Marketing. Here was my first big, flashing red light career inflection point! Importantly, I realized it as a critical opportunity at the time. I was aware enough to grasp that this type of opportunity was not likely to come along again any time soon at this company. Even more importantly, I understood that in all likelihood, due to the importance of the role along with my still fairly young age and relative lack of experience, I would not automatically be considered, let alone selected, as the new VP…it was far from a given.

Rather than simply hope that fate would smile on me, I took the situation into my own hands and decided to craft a letter detailing all the value I had brought to the company in the years I had been there. I presented factual data on how I had become expert in the business as well as the industry the business competed in. I further explained that I had an intimate understanding of the company's products and how they were marketed and sold because I had performed both the sales and marketing roles successfully. I was respectful but persuasive in my arguments explaining why I was the best choice for VP of Sales & Marketing for the business. However, I in no way implied I was owed this promotion. I was not pouty or threatening.

Even though there were other people in the commercial organization who had more years of experience than me, no one had the breadth of experience I had in both sales and marketing. Additionally, no one had produced the broad range of positive results I had in terms of strategic planning, product development, marketing and sales. At the end of the day, the owner, Al Weatherhead, the former president and the new president, who was also my previous boss, all agreed that I was the logical choice for the VP role. I was offered the position, thereby achieving my "VP by 33" goal at the age of 32.

Later, I was told by the former president of the business that the company had indeed been going down the path of recruiting the VP from the outside. He further acknowledged that my persuasive letter was the difference maker in considering and, ultimately, selecting me.

Life Hack #18: Inflection points can serve as warp-speed drives for your career and in helping you build wealth. In the example above, once I became a VP of sales and marketing, instantly, other companies naturally considered me for their VP roles.

By capitalizing on that one inflection point, I was able to put myself in a whole new strata of opportunities that would carry forward for the rest of my career. The likelihood of some other company considering me for a VP role, had I not secured this promotion, would have been difficult and a bit of a long shot. Bottom line: pay attention for these

types of inflection points in your own career and when they come along, put the time and effort into figuring out a way to capitalize on them!

How can you leverage your career inflection points?

- First, pay attention for when inflection points are happening. They usually don't come with a flashing red sign that says, "inflection point: pay attention!"
- Be ready to take action to make your case while the inflection point is still live and open for discussion. It's no time to procrastinate or be shy!
- It's also no time to be lazy. The time and effort you put in at these critical junctures to effectively make your case are literally worth gold.
- When you make your case, be prepared to respond if you get a positive response. Also be ready to negotiate! Know your "ask" if the opportunity comes along. Don't be a deer in the headlights and just say, "OK I accept" when offered the job. You must be prepared to negotiate for a fair and equitable deal for yourself and your family.

You will recall from earlier in the book, when I was figuring out what I wanted for a career while in college, I had made the firm decision that I absolutely did not want to go into sales. At the time, sales seemed like it was beneath me, as I had this mistaken stereotypical view that sales was kind of sleazy, cold-calling work that foisted stuff on people who didn't really want it.

I realized early in my career it was important for me to accept coaching and feedback. One of the most important inputs I received was from the president of the business where I worked. He told me during one of my reviews that he thought my career would benefit from me getting sales experience and having more direct interactions with the customer. I could have just nodded my head respectfully, and in my own mind still thought, "hell no, I know what's best for me and I'm not going to go into sales." Instead, I took his feedback to heart and started getting myself included in sales calls with our customers and, lo and behold, what I came to find is that professional business-to-business sales is not the slippery cold-calling hell I thought it was! Rather, it was actually a very exciting, dynamic, and interesting part of the business. As my career progressed over the following years I often had both sales and marketing management responsibilities. During this time, I found I actually loved the sales side far more than I had initially thought I would as a college student; in which I believed marketing was the more "sophisticated" part of the commercial process.

Life Hack #19: Be a learning creature: don't close your mind off to new opportunities based on your preconceived notions. Gladly accept constructive feedback from those trying to help your career. Had I not taken the "get some sales experience" advice to heart, I never would have gone on those sales calls, which led me to take a lateral sales role a few years later. Moreover, I wouldn't have had that broad sales and marketing experience when the inflection point came along that made me the best candidate for my first VP role.

While there is no precise roadmap for career inflection points, there are some typical situations that can often create the environment for inflection points to occur. These include:

- Internal promotions, especially when your manager is moving up.
- When a business is being acquired or spun off.
- When a new business unit within a company is being created.

You should always be working to develop relationships with those above and around you in a genuine (not patronizing) way. This shows you really want to learn and grow in the business. More often than not, especially with today's sometimes entitled, self-absorbed work force, those qualities and interests will help you stand out from the crowd, and those above you will more than likely want to be helpful to you by providing genuine guidance and support in your career.

Hire and retain the best talent

Another key in building a successful career is having success in hiring and developing people. Sometimes the biggest obstacle to you being promoted is that there is no one to take your place. In the worst possible irony, you've put a ceiling over your own advancement because you've made yourself indispensable in your current role... don't let that happen!

Out of paranoia, weak managers sometimes intentionally hire people who they feel can never compete with them for their current role. That's usually a sign the manager lacks confidence in their own ability and skills, so they defend their position by hiring dolts who can never take their current role away from them. If that's your outlook and mindset, chances are this book will be of little help to you.

Hiring and retaining people can be counter-intuitive in a certain sense. You actually want to hire people who are smarter than you, so that not only does the function you manage benefit, but you also have the ability to learn from them. It also provides a deep enough bench in your department so that there is never a question whether you can move up to a higher-level role without the perceived risk of your department, or function, not having someone who can take over for you.

In addition, there is no better advertisement within a company of your management ability than if you have a team that is always being sought out by other departments and getting promoted into other roles. That not only helps those individuals who are getting promoted but it also makes working on your team an attractive option for others in the organization because they see those people on your team advancing. All the while it makes you a star to those higher in the organization.

Also, once you achieve a high level role and are making a decent amount of money, few things are more gratifying than seeing those you hired and helped develop move on to great careers. There are many folks who have worked for me in the past who are now successful VPs. That fills me with a lot of pride and satisfaction. After the pandemic, the above skills will be even more important because finding and keeping talented folks will be more challenging than ever.

Avoid the natural tendency of cloning yourself!
There's another important element of hiring and recruiting that I learned early on in my career, it's the natural tendency in business and management for "self-replication"...to hire clones of yourself. This is not necessarily racist or intentional. It often happens at a sub-conscious level. It's human nature that we generally like ourselves, so it's natural to try to surround ourselves with people who think and act as we do. The big problem with this practice is that if everyone on your team has the same world view, and approaches problems and opportunities in the same way, you limit your potential for higher value-added solutions.

Somewhat paradoxically, I have found it is always best to *intentionally* try to hire and surround yourself with people who are significantly *different* than you...and not just to check a "woke" diversity box. Having your team made up of people with different life experiences and world views will help you consistently come up with a wider range of solutions to problems and opportunities. And when I say different I mean, judge people by their character, capability, and actual performance. Diversity for the sake of diversity, to check boxes, can be in itself, racism/sexism and whatever other ism you want to throw at it. Hire for attitude, motivation, and capability, and forget the rest. This may require you to push your HR team so they develop a broader range of candidates for you to consider. That's their job, so push them!

You are in business to make money and win, not check boxes. Look for people who think differently and have different interests than you do… even if that introduces some stress into your organization. That stress often results in better, more well-rounded solutions and allows you and your team to see around corners in this chaotic, ever-changing world better than a team with one group-think view.

Life Hack #20: Hire the best people, but intentionally seek out those who actually view the world differently than you do. This is reflected in their interests, what they studied, and what their aspirations are. As problems and opportunities arise, people with differing views, will help your organization arrive at a better, broader range of solutions.

Chapter 9

How Do You Negotiate Your Best Deal?

Negotiating early in your career

Early in most careers, the external roles you will be considered for, or the internal jobs you might be promoted into, typically have a narrowly predefined band of compensation and benefits. While it's important for you to know your worth in terms of compensation for each role you consider, there may be some perks you can negotiate beyond basic compensation. The reality is the employer will want to keep your compensation in this narrow band so that it doesn't distort the compensation for others doing similar work at your level. The more people there are working at the same level of the organizational pyramid you work in, the more rigid the compensation package will likely be.

However, we have seen that since the pandemic, in order to attract talent, employers have had to raise pay scales and get more creative with the perks they offer, even for entry level positions (for example, restaurants offering bonuses in return for workers staying a minimum number of months). Employers will typically offer identical incentives to everyone at the same level of the organization, so these benefits are still pretty fixed.

For those starting an entry level role right out of college, there may be some latitude negotiating the starting salary. If the role requires relocation, you may also be able to negotiate a better relocation package, such as a bigger lump sum payment in addition to covering moving expenses.

As noted, the variability in comp and benefits for a given role often comes down to how many others in that organization do similar work…the more there are, typically, the less flexibility there will be in the compensation package. As such, there might be more flexibility in a smaller organization to adjust comp, even for lower level roles, than in a larger company.

Negotiating is critical when you climb higher in the pyramid!

Once you've made progress climbing the ladder, and are offered a position in a more senior role, you need to be really thoughtful about negotiating the deal before accepting the position. The higher you rise in an organization, the more elements of your total compensation plan become negotiable. This is where you need to have broader knowledge beyond just the salary in terms of what's possible and what things you might consider.

Generally, when you are being considered internally or externally for a position where the title includes the word "manager," and certainly when the title contains "director" or "vice president," you will need to think through the total compensation package that is possible.

Do you know your market value?

There can be a significant divergence in what's possible from a comp standpoint if you are an internal candidate vs an external candidate. It may be contrary to your logic or sense of fairness, but the reality is companies will often pay more to hire an outside candidate than they will pay to promote an internal candidate to fill the same role. This happens, typically, because the company does not want to distort their established salary bands by paying a larger than normal increase (for example, paying more than a 10% increase in base salary for a promotion) to an internal candidate to fill a role. At the same time, the company can rationalize paying a "market competitive" salary that may be significantly higher for an eternal candidate.

The above scenario, which I've seen happen countless times in the companies I've worked for, is one of the reasons it is so critical for you to always ***be aware of your market value for the work you do.*** It is also why many recruiters will council you that you are sub-optimizing your value by staying with the same company for an extended part of your career. Internal promotions often will not keep pace, from a compensation standpoint, the same way changing companies for the same types of promotions often will. In addition, after a number of years, recruiters may simply stop reaching out to you if they feel you are "dead wood" and will not seriously consider leaving your longtime employer.

How can you keep track of what you're worth?

Based on the above, you hopefully understand that an important part of managing your career involves maintaining an understanding of the value of your skills and experience. To do this, try to keep track of what's going on from a published salary survey standpoint regarding compensation ranges and annual pay increases in your specific profession and industry, if possible. LinkedIn along with industry/trade publications are often good resources for this type of information. Joining LinkedIn groups for your industry/profession is a good place to start. For example, in the packaging industry where I spent most of my career, there are dozens of LinkedIn groups that I could potentially join. Use this knowledge to prepare for your performance reviews as well as when you begin considering external opportunities. For example, for many years, a typical annual 2-3% merit increase has been the norm in most large companies. However, given the recent return to Jimmy Carter era inflation, a 2% increase will likely be a thing of the past.

In addition, I strongly recommend developing relationships with professional recruiters who focus on your profession and/or industry. These folks only get paid when they place people in new roles so they know the market as well as anyone.

Whether you are preparing for an internal performance review, or you are interviewing for a new external role, knowing your market value will help you prepare and negotiate a reasonable outcome. In addition, for your internal reviews, always come armed with all the objective value you've brought to the business over the past year, and have an adult professional conversation about your worth. Most bosses will respect your preparation and ability to discuss this in an objective (not emotional!) way.

The number of compensation elements expand as you rise

A few years after I was promoted into my first VP role, I was approached by a recruiter with a new VP opportunity in a completely different industry. I explored the opportunity because it was local, didn't require a relocation, and was honestly the first time someone really aggressively recruited me for such a high level position.

As I did my due diligence during the recruitment process, I discovered the compensation package the new company was offering was way above the compensation I was currently being paid. This was my first exposure to the fact that moving up within the same company isn't always optimal from a compensation standpoint!

The new company was offering not only a dramatically higher salary but also a much more lucrative annual bonus plan as well as a long term bonus and an annuity that, after so many years, would pay me for the rest of my life. I was honestly shell shocked at how much better this deal was compared to the one I had with the company I had worked for since graduating college. I decided it was too good of a deal to turn down, so I verbally accepted it. Prior to signing the new employment agreement, I set up a discussion with my boss to tell him I would be leaving and to work out a transition time to exit.

My boss was literally shocked. Since I had been at this company my entire professional career, I don't think he ever thought I would go elsewhere. My boss called in his boss as well as the owner of the company, and they all asked me to give them a few days before I officially accepted the other offer. Much to my surprise, they came back the next day and apologized for the compensation they had been paying me. In essence, my bosses said that in hindsight, they had taken advantage of my tenure and were not paying me a market competitive rate. They offered a new compensation package that was better than the new offer I had and asked me to reconsider staying.

Warning: Inflection Point!

Here, my friends, I encountered one of those inflection point decisions I mentioned in the last chapter: Do I honor my word and accept the new company's offer, or do I accept the better offer from my current employer? Staying with my current employer would be the safer choice. I knew the company and industry and had good success and momentum in growing the business there. Accepting the new job would be risky because I knew nothing about the new company or their industry. At the same time, I wondered if my relationship with my current employer would be the same after they knew I went out and looked for another job?

Ultimately, I agreed to stay with my current employer. As is so often the case (and highlighted earlier in **Life Hack #3)** the easy decision, staying with my current employer, was not ethically the right decision; I went back on my word with the prospective new employer. While I ended up staying at my old company a few more years after this incident, it was never quite the same. Neither the management nor I ever viewed our relationship with the same level of trust. Over the next few years, I decided not only that I needed to leave this company but I also wanted to learn a new industry and have a different challenge.

Moving out of your comfort zone

One of my big take aways from the above experience was how unprepared I was, from a negotiating standpoint, when I received the new company's offer. I had no idea an actual employment contract, an annuity, or a long term bonus program were even elements I could negotiate on. When I finally decided to change jobs a few years later, I knew I needed to educate myself in order to understand what was possible from a compensation package standpoint. I certainly realized this job change would be an important new inflection point and sought outside knowledge to help me optimize the opportunity.

It's hard and, in a lot of cases, not socially appropriate to talk about compensation matters such as these with your peers. Frankly, a lot of my peers at that time were still in much lower level positions in their organizations and these types of scenarios weren't currently on the radar for them.

However, I did find a book that was an excellent resource. It became my road map for thinking through the various aspects of the negotiation I would subsequently have in finalizing the deal I would sign with my new company. That book was called "Perks and Parachutes: Negotiating Your Best Possible Employment Deal, from Salary and Bonus to Benefits and Protection" written by John Tarrant with Paul Fargis. This book was originally published in 1985, but had just been updated in 1997, the year in which I ended up making this career move.

Moving to greener pastures

In 1995 we had our first son. His birth influenced some of the priorities my wife and I had in our lives. Prior to having our son, my wife had just completed her MBA and had a successful career as a manager with a Fortune 500 company. After he was born, our planned child care option fell through, and my wife ended up working out an arrangement with her employer to retain her management role on a part time basis. This proved to be a challenge. After a year or so of juggling it, she was confronted with having to make the choice of going back full time, or leaving. She opted to leave.

At the same time, I was expanding my search to do something different. I was not only tired of working for the same company I had now worked at for more than 10 years but I also wanted the challenge of a different industry. Also, I was interested in moving somewhere else.

Early in 1997, I was approached with an opportunity to join a fast growing, family owned business in the Chicago area that competed in the electronics industry. The founder of this company had grown the business from scratch over the last twenty years. He was looking to transition management to his son, who was the company's CFO, and to a newly created VP of Sales and Marketing role. The goal was to transition the management in order take the business successfully into the future. This position checked all the boxes of what I was considering for a new role. Although it was risky in many ways (new company, new industry, new city, etc.), I really liked the people I'd met who worked there. The job seemed like a great fit for my skill set. It was also an opportunity to try out the things I had learned about negotiating a comprehensive employment deal.

What's important in your deal?

Because this company was relatively small (under $50 million in sales at the time), the role was a newly created position, and I was negotiating directly with the owner of the business (no other decision makers involved), the potential existed to negotiate on a wide range of compensation package elements. It was the perfect opportunity for me to apply the teachings from the book mentioned previously. We ended up agreeing on a deal that included:

- Base salary that was much higher than I was currently earning
- Full relocation, including my new employer agreeing to buy my current house if it did not sell within a certain amount of time
- Payment of all living expenses until my house was sold
- A significant signing bonus
- A Company car
- A guaranteed minimum bonus in my first year
- A long term incentive plan
- More vacation than I currently had
- An exit agreement in the event my position was terminated any time in the future other than for "cause"

- Other benefits such as insurance, holidays, and retirement programs

The book was really helpful not only in pointing out the possible elements of the compensation plan I might be able to negotiate but it also flagged "watch outs" for negotiating each of these. It even provided suggested language that I ended up incorporating in my final employment agreement, saving me a lot of legal costs.

Here are some brief comments on these various compensation elements describing what they are and what to pay attention to as you negotiate your best deal:

Base salary

- For internal promotions, my experience is that it can be difficult to secure more than a 10% increase in your base. This can be many times larger if you make the move to another company.

Relocation

- If you have to move for a new internal or external job, make sure you are being properly compensated for the move:
    - This typically includes payment of all actual move costs including paying to pack and unpack your goods.
    - Utility hookups.
    - Payment to move vehicles to the new location.
    - Typically a lump sum payment for miscellaneous costs.
    - All transaction costs for the sale of your old house and the purchase of your new house including real estate commissions and closing costs on loans.
    - Costs for one or more house hunting trips to the new location for you and your spouse.

- Combined, these relocation costs can reach six figures for an executive move so it's really important your employer agrees to "gross up" all the costs so that they pay all the income taxes associated with these reimbursements because they count as taxable income. Otherwise, you could be stuck holding the bag for tens of thousands of dollars in income taxes.

- Important, if you don't have a house to sell or buy as part of this relocation, you are saving your employer boat loads of money. You could be nice and let them keep that money or you could use that to your advantage and negotiate a portion of that savings for yourself. Given relocation is a one time cost, your employer will probably not want to increase your ongoing base pay to compensate but they might be open to paying a (bigger) signing bonus. For example, if you estimate their total savings related to your not selling or buying a house is $75,000, you might ask for a $50,000 signing bonus instead. It's a win-win!

- Living expenses paid until your relocation is complete. Make sure you specify what are reasonable accommodations. When I made my move to Chicago, I stipulated a two bedroom, two bath apartment so it would be comfortable for my family to live there, not just me. Had I not included this language, the employer may have only offered to reimburse me for a studio apartment.

Signing bonus

- This is a great element to include in the package as a "compromise" in the event you and the employer can't quite come to terms on the base salary.

    - A signing bonus is easier for the employer to rationalize because it's only a one time hit.

- You can also sometimes negotiate a signing bonus to de-risk the potential for not knowing how your bonus might pay out in year 1.

- I've never known an employer to proactively offer a signing bonus, but in every negotiation where I have asked for one, I've gotten one. So don't be afraid to constructively throw this on the table at the right time!

Company car

- This perk used to be somewhat of a norm, especially if you were in sales but it's not the case anymore. There are typically two ways this type of incentive can be offered:

  - The traditional way is the company provides you a car and directly pays for the lease cost, gas, insurance, and the maintenance. The car is typically replaced every 2-3 years.

  - Today, the more typical way is the company will provide a car allowance where they agree to pay you a certain amount per month. You are then responsible for buying and maintaining the car. Generally, the only reimbursement you get is for the business mileage you incur.

  - With the traditional option your car style choices are usually limited, but it's by far the best way to go from a compensation standpoint because you are not taxed when the company pays for everything. With the car allowance option, you are W-2'd for the amount they pay you each month.

Minimum first year bonus

- The higher up you go in an organization, the more important bonus programs are as a percent of your total compensation. Given the risk of you not really knowing the new company you are joining, or how bonuses are actually paid, it is often perceived as a fair request that you be guaranteed to earn a minimum bonus the first year, regardless of your actual bonus performance. If the bonus has a "target" payout level, this is often a reasonable amount to agree upon.

Long term incentive plans

- These plans typically require you to remain an active employee for a vesting period, usually three years.
- After the initial vesting period, you earn a long term bonus payout each year as each subsequent year vests. These are sometimes referred to as "golden handcuffs" because once you start accruing these payouts, it can be hard to leave from a financial standpoint.
- There are many variations in how long term incentive plans work:
- It can be as simple as your long term award for a given year equals 50% of your annual bonus for that year and is paid in company stock when it vests.
- It can also be based on the company achieving overall metrics over the vesting period like earnings per share and paid out using more complex formulas.
- There can also be multiple compensation elements in the long term plan such as restricted stock units and/or stock options. These are all good things but it is important you understand what these elements are and how much they are worth. It's an important consideration if, at some point, you consider leaving that company to know clearly how much future compensation you might be walking away from.
- These types of plans are usually very well defined for each position/level in the organization and generally are not negotiable. The only thing you might be able to negotiate is how soon you can participate in the plan. For example, there may be

a general rule that you need to be employed for one year before you can start participating. You may be able to negotiate being included in the plan your first year. It can't hurt to ask!

Vacation

- You never want to lead a comp plan negotiation focusing on how much vacation you will get…it's bad form and sends the wrong message about your work ethic. That being said, once you have the major elements of the agreement hammered out, it's important to discuss how much vacation you will receive.

  - Most companies have etched in stone vacation policies that will apply to all new hires, regardless of the level of your role.

  - The last thing you will want if you've been working for 20 years and have four weeks of vacation earned is to go back to having just two weeks per year!

  - I have found the best way to raise this topic is when you actually put together a written response to the employer's offer. Usually this takes place after base, bonus, and other key elements of the comp plan have been agreed upon.

  - At that point you can simply insert, "4 weeks of paid vacation per year until superseded by company policy" in your counter proposal.

  - If the company questions this, you can just say this is to maintain your current benefit level. In most cases, it won't be an issue. Like other elements noted above, if you don't ask you may end up with the standard company policy benefit. So ask!

Exit & non-compete agreements

- If you've worked for the same company for your entire career, you've likely never thought about the need for an exit agreement.

The reality is, in such a situation, you are stuck getting whatever the company decides it will give you if they decide to terminate you.

- When you are negotiating with a new employer, the higher the level your role, the more important it is to secure a fair exit deal. Companies get bought and sold all the time and if your new employer divests the business in the future, the higher you are in their organization, the more likely it is you will find yourself out of a job.

    - Try to secure at least 6 months compensation following the company's termination of your employment for anything other than "cause." Make sure "cause" is clearly defined in the agreement to mean stealing or breaking the law during the course of your employment, it shouldn't, in any way, be based on your performance or the results you produced.

    - The severance payment should be based on your highest monthly base salary (so they can't demote you, cut your pay, and then terminate you! Yes that happens).

    - The compensation should be paid regardless of whether you find new employment elsewhere during the agreed severance period (yes, companies try to do that!).

    - Include in your negotiation that the company will continue to pay your medical benefits during the severance payment period.

- In addition, many employers will want you to sign a non-compete agreement should you decide in the future to leave them, or even if they terminate you. It's a reasonable request that if the employer wants you to sign such an agreement they provide consideration in the form of exit compensation to cover you during your time of transition if they terminate you.

Even with a severance agreement, always work to limit the scope of the non-compete as narrowly as you can. If you're in sales this is particularly important: don't sign an agreement that broadly restricts you from selling to your current customers or, even worse, to the market you are known in. At most, limit the agreement to not selling specifically defined products which directly compete with your employer for a limited amount of time...ideally 6 months and no more than one year.

Other benefits

- As you progress through the negotiation, it's a good idea to ask your counterpart to have the HR department send you the company's benefits manual. It will typically include general employment information on vacation, paid holidays, and retirement benefits such as a pension (rare), or 401k (typical). You will want to study this information to determine how these benefits compare to your current employer's. You might find, as I did in my last job, that the 401k match was actually much better than my prior employer provided. You can then factor that into your overall evaluation of the total package.

Life Hack #21: Learn the art of negotiation...it can dramatically improve your ability to grow wealth over the course of your career. While I have included some key points in this chapter to help, there is a wealth of information out there on negotiating strategy and skills, including the book I referenced.

Life Hack #22: Negotiating 101-Here are some high level tips:

- **Whether you are negotiating a sale, to buy a car or house, or negotiating for your next job, always try to get the other side's offer first! They may make a better offer than you would have dreamed of asking for. If you offer your number first, you've just put a ceiling on the amount you will earn. Don't do it!**

- **Embrace the silence! Often the most important parts of a negotiation whether in person, on the phone, or on a zoom call, are the pauses...where each side is waiting for the other side to say something. Be disciplined and try to let the other side speak. Don't be afraid of the sometimes uncomfortable silences that will occur in any negotiation. This is often when the other side will make a concession but if they are an experienced negotiator, they will want to see if you blink first.**

- **Be aware of your body language. Make sure your facial mask is calm and has a confident, positive expression.**

- **Emotional attachment to the deal is your enemy! In any important negotiation (making a sale, negotiating for a new job, or buying a new house or car), determine the minimum terms you must have for you to agree to the deal BEFORE you start the negotiation. You must be willing to walk away from the negotiation and feel good about yourself if you don't secure your predetermined minimum acceptable deal. This mindset will be evident in your persona and body language when you are bargaining and conveys non-verbally to the other side you are not bluffing. The other side will realize that if they want to conclude the deal, they must agree to your minimum terms. If you don't come to terms, you can walk away knowing you made the right decision. There is always another deal, job, house, or car out there!**

Chapter 10

"You Incorporated" Part 1-Earning!

Is building wealth a priority for you?

The following "You Incorporated" chapters are intended to help put you in the driver's seat of building wealth over the course of your life without needing to pay a financial advisor.

As a reminder, the observations and suggestions in this book are my opinions based on my experience and are intended for education and information purposes. While I provide the basics of investing along with some strategies and examples of possible investments, **the information I present is *not* intended as financial advice or recommendations for specific investments**. The future is unknown, nowadays more than ever, so nothing is guaranteed. Use this information as a baseline and go learn more, then once you feel comfortable, make your own decisions and own the results.

I titled the next four chapters "You Incorporated" because, in reality, that's what you are: from a professional and financial standpoint, you are your own business entity. The choices you make will impact your personal bottom line.

I think there is value in having a "You Incorporated" mindset for managing your career and wealth-building activities. You can choose to sell your services to some other company that pays you a wage or you can strike out on your own and create your own business. You can also do, as more and more people after the pandemic are finding, some combination of both. Likewise, you can choose to manage your investment activities yourself "in-house," or farm these services out and pay an investment advisor.

Regardless of which way you go, you own you, and also the results/outcomes of how successful your efforts are. The worst thing you can do, in pretty much any aspect of your life, is to not own/take responsibility for the results and outcomes of your choices and efforts. Doing so risks setting up a never-ending mental cycle of why "you are the victim" as an explanation for why things didn't go your way. If you are currently in the habit of doing that, STOP! You will be hard pressed to find a successful individual in any walk of life who didn't own their mistakes and shortcomings. It's the only way you will ever address the issues that are holding you back head-on, and be able to improve. Embrace setbacks and "failures" as these are really opportunities in disguise, which allow each of us to understand and address our shortcomings.

Life Hack #23: Winners don't cry and blame society, their upbringing, or the other guy. Winners accept the reality of their situation, including the reality that life isn't always fair, they suck it up, figure out a way to overcome the obstacles they encounter, and move on to bigger and better things.

The 3 levers you use to build wealth

Now that you have the proper mindset, there are three primary levers you can pull to grow your wealth during the course of your life. I call these **Earning, Burning, and Churning** and I will cover each of these topics in the next three chapters. Here's a brief description to start:

Earning-Barring a rich relative dying or winning the lottery, this is your main wealth-building lever, especially early in your career. "Earning" can be the wage you get paid working for someone else or the profits you generate from working on your own. Unfortunately, for those who do too much "Burning" (see below), earning can remain your primary wealth building input through much of your career as well.

Burning-This is the act of taking your hard earned dinero and

"Burning" (spending) it on low or no ROI (return on investment) items...some of these items are needs (food, basic shelter, etc.), but much of what we spend money on in our modern society are wants. For example, the new boat, imported car, and/or house that's more shelter than what you really need. It's also the little things that add up, like that $5 latte every morning.

Churning-Like turning cream into butter, "Churning" is all about learning how to turn the valuable assets you currently have (cash in the bank, property, stocks, bonds, crypto currency, etc.) into more valuable assets over the course of time. At a basic but actionable level, I will explain the fundamentals of how to build wealth. Here's the big secret: learning how to consistently grow your wealth is not rocket science. Just about anyone can learn and use the concepts I will share without paying a financial advisor a percent or two of their wealth every year to manage their money. While it doesn't sound like a lot, that 1-2% will significantly eat into your wealth building over your career.

Life Hack #24: Your goal should be to transition as soon as you can during your career from relying on "earning" to "churning" in order to build your wealth. The key ways to build wealth, especially early in your career, are to reduce your rate of "burning" through the moolah, and to increase your rate of "earning."

In addition, establishing the right habits and strategies for "churning"/investing your small but growing pile of money early in life is also very important to get the churning lever working for you. Once I hit my "millionaire by 40" goal, one of my next big financial goals was, by age 50, to get my investment portfolio to where it was generating more wealth each year than I was by working. In other words I wanted my churning lever to be making more money than my earning lever. By achieving that goal, I was able to put myself on a solid path towards building the wealth

necessary to retire when I chose. The steps I outline in these chapters can allow you to do the same thing.

Earning:

First, let's start with making the dough. How do you maximize your earnings? I will outline some things I've learned along the way that will hopefully help but some of the building blocks, in terms of your career and negotiating, have already been discussed earlier in this book.

As noted in previous chapters, the best way to set yourself up for future earnings success is to carefully think through what you want to do with your life and get the appropriate training (be that through college, trade school, or self-taught through the myriad online resources that exist today). Use the power and magic of goal setting and get in the habit of laying out what you really want to accomplish. This includes setting specific short, medium, and long term goals that outline, **in writing,** how much you want to earn, how you expect your wealth to grow over time, and where you expect to be in your career at given points in the future. For example, I would typically set 1, 3, 5, and 10 year goals in most of the Personal Inventory categories noted earlier in the book.

Early in your career, setting a goal for how much you want to be earning 5, let alone 10, years out is a wild guess. My recommendation is to aim high and write the goal down…there is magic in a written goal, as stated earlier. Then, review, reflect on, and refine those goals regularly to ensure you are on track.

Use the "Personal Inventory" tools described in Chapter 4 to monitor your progress on all critical aspects of your life and to ensure you are staying well balanced…**remember at the end of the day, the goal is sustained happiness, not zeros on a piece of paper!** Finally, as I discussed in Chapter 8, always be on the lookout for inflection points in your career. Taking full advantage of these can rocket your career trajectory quickly.

The process of growing your earnings over time during your career is a dynamic process..."you own you," and you most certainly own making the most out of your chosen career. If you leave things to chance and just rely on "fate" for good things to happen, you won't maximize your potential.

- Assess your boss and his or her boss. Ask yourself, what makes them tick, and how can I add value to help them achieve their goals?
- What's really going on in your business? Look beyond your specific role and tasks. Really try to understand the dynamics that help or hurt your department and the broader business. The quicker you understand these things, the more likely you will be able to develop meaningful ways to help, and this has the potential to get you noticed in a positive way. I'm all about results; not BS or fluff.
- Do you have ideas that can contribute to increased sales and/or reduced costs, and thereby improved profit?
- You only get one life...make the most of your opportunities with passion and integrity and the earnings will surely follow!

Is it time for you to make a change?

Businesses and people change over time. At some point, if you aren't satisfied with "You Inc.'s" income or where you're at in your career, you can:

1. **Get another job...as in a second, third or fourth job.** These are known today as "Slash" careers. It's becoming much more common to have multiple streams of income, and not just for the youngsters starting out. Pursuing this route (either with a full-time main job and other part time "moonlighting" gigs, or with multiple part-time gigs) has benefits in terms of flexibility and work stability (you are unlikely to lose multiple jobs at the same time). It also helps you gain multiple, diverse, career

learning experiences, which may accelerate your career progression.

The downside to this option is that juggling multiple jobs can increase stress, reduce time for family or personal interests, and may not allow you to focus enough time to maximize the opportunities at your primary job.

2. **Get another job...as in switching from your current job to another one that pays more money and/or offers better career progression potential.** In my father's generation, the norm was to stay with one company for most, if not all, of your career because company pensions helped cement that commitment with the proverbial golden handcuffs.

The days of company pensions are largely gone (although Covid and the change in the axis of power between employers and employees may change that down the road!), so it's a pretty unique situation where you would maximize your potential working for one company your entire career today. That is unless you work for one of those giant, dinosaur employers still out there that don't actually have to compete, known as government/public sector employers.

In my generation, changing careers was not only common, it was generally regarded as the smart move to maximize your career earnings. Moves every 3-7 years were/are fairly typical. Recruiters I've known and worked with for many years would say a person is sub-optimizing their earnings if they stay too long with one employer. In addition, a person potentially gets viewed as "dead wood" by prospective employers when they stay at one employer for too long, especially if that person has been in the same role for several years.

For younger generations, including millennials and Gen Z'ers, if an employee isn't being offered some avenue for growth in opportunity and/or earnings every year or two, that person is likely to leave for greener pastures.

As a result, in just a few generations, the employee's perspective has gone from "life-long loyal servant appreciative to have a job" in my dad's generation, to "keep me constantly motivated, moving upward with ever increasing pay and satisfaction, or I am out of here," in the current generation.

None of these career approaches are right or wrong and they are really largely reactions to what employers, on their side of the table, are providing. In your career, it is important to be sensitive to each generation's mindset. Use empathy; put yourself in your boss's skin to help understand their worldview and anticipate their reactions.

If you are a millennial, and you change jobs three times in four years, the baby boomers reviewing your background for that next opportunity might toss your resume simply for changing jobs too quickly, and that can stall your career. There is a good rationale for this: it takes a fair amount of time and money to onboard a new employee and get them to the point of actually being productive for the business. Having an employee only stay 1-2 years is not a winning proposition for the manager, or the company. Granted, the manager and employer have some ownership in this by providing a work environment that incentivizes people to stay, but this dynamic can be a real challenge these days.

The reality, in my experience, is the longer you are with a given company, especially if you are not being promoted on a somewhat regular basis (every 2-4 years), the chances are high that you are drifting below market-level compensation. You need to be actively keeping a toe in the water, understanding not only what other opportunities are out there but also what the market-level compensation is for your current job.

Establish symbiotic relationships with recruiters: Developing ongoing relationships with professional recruiters in your industry can be very beneficial to you. They can not only keep you aware of new job opportunities but also provide you with feedback on current comp trends for someone with your experience. In turn, you can help them from time to time by providing leads for candidates in searches that might not be a fit for you.

3. **Work harder/longer and earn a raise or promotion.** If you are paid by the hour, or your pay is based on output /piecework, or you want to show you are worth more money, put in more effort and time, and produce more measurable results.

While I'm not a fan of coming in early and working late just for the "appearance/show" value of this for your boss, I have not met a lot of successful people who got to the top working a 40 hour week. Most successful people I've known bust their ass and do what it takes to get the job done right, and they do this with passion and out of a competitive desire to be the best as well as to get ahead.

There is a fantastic book called Outliers by Malcolm Gladwell (see the reference section at the back of the book for details) that explores the underlying roots of excellence in many different careers. One of the conclusions in this fascinating book is that across many different fields of interest, a common denominator is you've got to put in the time to master excellence. Gladwell uses the 10,000 hours number in his book as a threshold for this. But whether you want to become an expert soccer player, a professional guitarist, or the best marketer in your selected industry, there is no substitute for putting in the time to have your brain grow and evolve from that experience. The quicker you get your "10,000 hours" in versus those you are competing against, the bigger your edge will be over them in the marketplace and in climbing the ladder.

I gave Outliers to my younger son around the age of 14. He was just starting his music production business using Garage Band in his room to create beats or melodies that he would then try to market/ license online. At the time, he was also playing several sports. The book really helped galvanize his passion for the music business. He was fortunate to find his passion so early in life and he became determined to get his "10,000 hours" in while still in high school.

Eventually, despite being a decent athlete, he gave up high school sports so he could allocate more time to his passion. He read every book he could get his hands on related to music intellectual property, took courses to master social media marketing, and gained experience producing melodies.

By the time he moved to Nashville to devote his full efforts to growing his music production and management business, at age 19, he was already, in many ways, a seasoned pro. The point of this story is not to just brag on my son (ok, maybe a little of it is that) he's unique in some ways and was certainly more driven as a teenager than I ever was. The point is, you have to put in the time and effort if you really want to climb the ladder quickly in whatever career or business you choose to pursue.

One of the advantages of working with and competing against today's somewhat self-absorbed newer workers is that you will very likely stand out from the herd if you are putting in extra time and, most importantly, producing extraordinary results. Many of your peers will be working the bare minimum. It used to be the opposite when I was starting out. Everyone largely put in extra time, even if just for appearance's sake, and you stood out (in a bad way) if you were the one leaving at 5pm on the dot.

Life Hack #25: While your job description might say, "office hours are from 8-5 with one hour for lunch," the reality is few become successful working a 40 hour week. Other than relying on luck, there are no substitutes for putting in the time, not only to produce extraordinary results in your current role but also to become truly expert in your line of work. Here's where choosing to do something you really like and are passionate about comes into play: if that's the case, you often won't notice how many hours you are putting in!

4. **Work smarter and review your ladder climbing skills.** Maybe some assessment of how you are going about moving up in your organization will help you adjust and accelerate. To repeat; be a learning creature and determine:

   - What are the personalities and the culture in your work environment?
   - What makes your boss and others above him or her tick?
   - How are they motivated and incentivized?

As noted in Life Hack #10 in Chapter 6, empathize with those above and around you not only to be a caring person but also to understand how you fit, and how you might be going against the grain in terms of how you are working and interacting with your boss and others.

This is not to say you should be a "suck up," I am simply advising that how you act impacts how you progress. To the extent your personality is fully aligned and supports all of your boss's hopes and wishes as they relate to the business, chances are, you are optimizing your ability to move up, **assuming you are producing results.**

Be a chameleon

Early in my career, I was blessed to work with a sage salesman who told me that to be a really successful salesperson, I needed to be a chameleon. What he meant by that is when you are sitting across the desk from someone, if you are a learning creature, you will pick up cues from their office, family pictures, awards, diplomas, etc. that provide insight as to what is important to that person. When you listen to them, you get a sense for not only what their priorities are but also how they express them.

To the extent you can adapt your persona and communication style to not conflict with these attributes, you put yourself in a much better position to connect with that person. Again, we are not talking about bullshitting or putting on a false face, like some northern politician talking with a southern drawl when addressing a black church in Alabama…that's patronizing. What I am talking about here is how you can best connect and be able to understand where the other person is coming from so you can effectively communicate with them. This doesn't just apply in sales with customers, it also applies with how you interact with people in your work environment.

For example, if you know your boss is a religious person who never swears, it wouldn't be a good move, despite how hard you are working and the results you are producing, if you're frequently dropping f-bombs and saying how stupid christians are. Doing so immediately makes your career ladder a much longer climb, even if this may have nothing to do with your work output. You don't have to fake-match your boss's interests, just don't poke him or her with things that you know go directly counter to their interests and beliefs.

Lead with a smile

Here's another simple thing that can help you in all settings, work or otherwise: lead with a smile. What I mean by this is that our natural expression in most new, stressful and/or work settings is a neutral or downcast one.

Teach yourself when being introduced to someone new, when joining a new group, or anytime your are meeting with a colleague, boss or work associate, to enter that discussion with a confident smile. This simple act (which requires some self-awareness and training on your part to get into the habit) will disarm those around you and make everyone feel more relaxed and comfortable. Importantly, it will broadcast to others that you are confident and comfortable in your own skin…and everyone wants to be like that and wants to be around people who are like that. If you are naturally predisposed to being shy or more introverted (as I used to be early in my career), leading with a smile can help you feel more confident from the get-go. In most interactions, your smiling will generally result in others smiling back at you which, in turn, will help your self-confidence at the outset of that interaction. Try it...what do you have to lose? Sometimes it's these simple habits and skills that can make the difference!

5. **Educate yourself to become qualified for a better paying job.** When I graduated with my BSBA from Ohio State, I found there were no marketing opportunities without an MBA. Based on that, I enrolled at the beginning of the following year in the full time MBA program at Case Western Reserve University. As your career progresses, you may find you need more training of one sort or another to be considered for a job you aspire to.

It's important to asses this situation carefully because, as I can tell you from experience, juggling this added training while working, especially if you have a family, requires significant time commitment and can introduce a lot of stress not only for you but also for those around you. Still, sometimes this choice is absolutely the right one. I certainly never would have achieved what I have in my career if I had not gone back for my MBA. It wasn't just the piece of paper (although, in my case, that piece of paper was a gatekeeper for certain roles), the bigger value was the concentrated learning I received in the MBA program that put me on another level, which would have taken many years of work experience to attain. The degree turbo charged my career.

6. **Start your own business.** With interconnectivity and the low cost internet-based tools and platforms that exist today, it has never been easier to start a business and have access to a global market. While you could start a traditional brick and mortar business, the opportunities to start an online business are almost limitless. In addition, the "how to" training for just about any type of business you might want to explore is also readily available on Youtube, podcasts, and other online resources. Like writing a book or starting any new venture, the hardest part is STARTING!

7. **7-Buy a Powerball ticket (just kidding).**

So, sit down and ask yourself if the money you are making and the earnings track you are on meet your short and long term requirements. If they do, great…you are on track. If they don't, what are you going to do about it? Remember: You Own You!

As you are reviewing your progress towards your goals, the above list of "Earning" options is one way to assess how you can skin the cat in a different way to get where you want to go, ideally faster. The bottom line is your goals need to align with your real potential short and long term earning power…otherwise you risk having your goals morph into dreams that will never be achieved.

Chapter 11

"You Incorporated" Part 2-Burning!

Now that you understand the elements as well as some options to put yourself on a good earnings trajectory, you need to manage the "holes" in your wealth bucket. While "Earning" and "Churning" each contribute to filling your wealth bucket, "Burning" (spending) empties it.

Burning, for many people, is the fun part. Spending money earned or borrowed on all those shiny things you've always wanted is awesomeness personified, right? Not always, the gratification obtained by spending is frequently a short-lived fix and can be a happiness mirage.

There is a fantastic book titled "Your Money or Your Life" (see additional details in the Suggested References section at the back of the book) that I wish I had read earlier in my life. Originally written in 1992, the book was a catalyst for the whole FIRE (Financially Independent Retire Early) movement. I read the recently updated edition of the book after reading a review of it in Money Magazine. While there are many great insights in this book and several practical steps are outlined to guide you in getting your spending under control, a key idea in the book that stuck with me and truly changed my life is the concept of ***"enoughness."***

My interpretation of enoughness is being aware, and intentional in every aspect of your life:

- When you are eating, enjoy the food, each bite of it.
- When you are full, stop eating even if there is still food left on your plate. You've had enough.

- When you are planning to buy something, think about the value of that item, be it a house, car, or shiny trinket that's an impulse purchase: is that item worth the "life energy" you gave up working to make the after tax money to buy it?

To me, the concept of "enoughness," though simple, was mind-blowing. The book explains how we are raised in a society that is driven to make each of us always want "more" even though "more" often times is actually bad for us. Using this conscious self-awareness is not automatic. If you are an old dog like me, just the simple act of focusing on enjoying each bite of food and listening to my body when I've had enough takes time and a lot of practice, but the results can be remarkable and your level of satisfaction with everything you apply this approach to will increase dramatically. Again, the secret is ***you control you.*** <u>You</u> can change the way you approach eating, spending, and living.

Had I read this book when it first came out in the early 90's, when I was still in my thirties, I might have made some course corrections in my career and done some things differently. As it happened, I read this book in late 2019 as I was pondering how much longer I wanted to do what I was doing to earn money (at the time, I was Senior Vice President for a large international packaging company).

When I applied the simple concepts outlined in the book to my financial situation, there was no doubt about it: I had built enough wealth to not have to work for another dollar ever again. I ran the numbers backwards and forwards, with various challenging assumptions like, for example, what if the market dropped 50%... would I be able to maintain my lifestyle? Every time, the answer came back the same: to do the things that are important to my wife and me, and to live the way we want to live, I did not have to keep working for money.

One of the things that provided confidence in this analysis was the fact I had been successfully managing my own investments for my whole adult life. This is one of the reasons I feel so strongly about the importance of you having a clear understanding of the basics of how to manage your money vs relying on someone you are paying a fee to tell you when it's ok for you to retire. Let's be honest: their compensation typically grows as your portfolio grows. Do they really want you to stop working and potentially start spending down your portfolio?

We are conditioned to work longer and want "MORE"

The decades old societal conditioning in my brain told me I needed to "work until I'm 65 and get on Medicare." My conditioning also told me I needed to work to "save more money on a piece of paper because the amount of money I have is less than some other people's"...how crazy is that when you stop and think about it!?

Again, **our society programs us to never be satisfied that we have "enough."** Upon some deep reflection after reading the book, I realized I had achieved "enoughness" from a financial standpoint. I could do all the things I really wanted to in life if I never earned another dollar working.

This was another mind-blowing moment. When you are raised to expect you will always be working to chase another $, and then you realize you can stop before you intended to, it raises some interesting and challenging questions. If I don't have to work for dollars, what do I really *want* to do? Confronting that question, my friends, is a blessing you will all want encounter one day because, as I am now finding out, that inflection point can open a whole new world and life for you!

As this relates to "Burning"...spending your hard earned dollars, one of the key things my wife and I did early in our marriage is we agreed on never spending more than we earned, and to try and have a lifestyle that was a bit below what we could afford. This simple approach to life and spending can have a dramatic impact on your wealth building power over your career.

What this means in practical terms is:

- You pay your credit cards in full each month.
- You don't need to max out on the size of house you purchase.
- You don't buy the fancy or always brand new car to impress your neighbors (really, is there any sadder symbol of your low self-esteem than when you compensate in this way?).
- We are also not big impulse buyers…neither of us likes a lot of clutter and, frankly, the older we've gotten, the more we actually get pleasure from unloading/decluttering/donating "stuff" than we do in buying more "stuff."

All of these things…the big and the little purchases… add up, so the quicker you establish good spending habits, the sooner you will start getting the "burning" aspect of wealth building working for you and not against you.

To manage the burn properly and on an ongoing basis, it means establishing a budget for your income and expenditures. The book I referenced earlier, Your Money or Your Life, provides really detailed examples of how to do this and how to make it work in simple terms. Essentially, you need to define all the ways you spend your money and determine what amount of your household income you can allocate to each type of spending. Try to figure out the bare minimum you need and really challenge yourself.

Setting up the budget is a great time to honestly assess where your money goes and if that is the best use of your hard earned money. If the total spending you come up with does not provide any leftover income to save and invest, you need to go back to the drawing board to figure out what expenses you can reduce or eliminate, or how you can earn more money. **To build wealth you have to develop a habit of spending less than you earn!**

Like your goals, write all this down or, better yet, set up a simple spreadsheet so you can enter your actual expenditures and track how you are doing. Tracking your actual expenditures and reviewing your income statement (total income less all your expenses) is key and, out of the gate, I suggest you do this, along with your spouse if you are married, every month.

Here is a simple budget example. The more detail you can add for different types of expenses the better. To track expenses, I created a Note on my iPhone and record expenses on it as I go through the month. Then I load these into the spreadsheet when time permits.

Expense	January Budget	January Actual	Over/Under Budget
Mortgage	$1,000.00	$1,000.00	$0.00
Food	$600.00	$500.00	-$100.00
Food Out	$200.00	$400.00	$200.00
Electric	$100.00	$90.00	-$10.00
Auto Expense	$500.00	$450.00	-$50.00
Cable	$150.00	$140.00	-$10.00
Cell Phone	$100.00	$110.00	$10.00
Entertainment	$100.00	$300.00	$200.00
Insurance	$200.00	$180.00	-$20.00
Other	$100.00	$50.00	-$50.00
Total:	$3,050.00	$3,220.00	$170.00

Initially, this might be an eye-opening and somewhat frustrating exercise but, over time, if you address the leaks in your bucket, you will make progress and start saving meaningful money most months. Yes, there will be times a car breaks down unexpectedly but even those types of expenses can be estimated and planned for. Using a budget allows you to gain control over the rate of burn and this control over your financial life is satisfying and stress-reducing. This simple discipline can be a huge difference maker over the course of your life.

My wife and I have been doing this budgeting process for virtually all of our marriage…it's become second nature. Here's the big side benefit. Many marriages end due to issues related to finances and, more specifically, spending. When you do this budgeting and tracking of expenditures together in an open, honest way, it largely takes money away as a point of conflict. You both worked on and agreed to the budget and you are both working to manage expenditures and savings. It turns the spending issue into an objective problem somewhat independent of each spouse: at the end of the day, if the savings are not being achieved, it means either the budget is impossible to live within, or (far more likely) you both collectively need to figure out how and where you are going to spend less. You attack the problem instead of each other for having too few dollars at the end of each month, and that's a really good thing.

Life Hack #26: Develop a budget! This is a key tool for managing your financial life and building wealth. In addition, being in control of your finances reduces stress and helps towards the goal of sustained happiness.

Here is a side benefit of this approach to spending and, frankly, living within your means in an intentional way: it will rub off on your kids. Include them in the process and let them see how you make budget and spending choices. You will be providing a responsible example and helping to set them up with better habits and to fully appreciate the blessings they have…be it a good meal or a nice toy…and not always immediately wanting more.

The "consume at all costs" addiction that is pumped into us by society really doesn't make us more fulfilled and doesn't really lead to the sustained happiness that, to me, is always the end game. By enjoying each thing you have and fighting the compulsion to always be looking for the next "thing," you'll make each day richer and more rewarding.

Life Hack #27: As the above book example's impact on my life hopefully shows, it can be really valuable to take the time to read some books. These can have the potential to change not only your outlook on specific topics but also maybe even the trajectory of your life. I've listed a handful of books such as "Your Money or Your Life" in the reference section at the back of this book.

While you can consume "books" in many ways today, to me, there is something magical and more valuable when you actually read a book vs simply listening to it, or watching a movie based on it. Your mind creates imagery and connections that only happen when you read. If you haven't read a book since school, give it a whirl…it will likely enhance your life.

Note: reading is like exercising a muscle…if you've not done it in a while, you are going to be a pretty slow reader. Have faith, with practice, you will quickly start reading faster and your brain will absorb more. Also, while the books I've listed in the back are all non-fiction works, there is huge value in reading both fiction and non-fiction. Many newbie readers only read non-fiction to their detriment. There are many excellent fiction writers who do incredible research on the topics they write about, and they bring these topics to life in a much more entertaining way than a potentially dry non-fiction work on the same subject.

Open your mind and feed your brain by reading…everyone around you will thank you as you will become a much

more interesting person to talk to! Also, like your spending habits, if you read for pleasure and knowledge, it will rub off on your kids, and maybe they won't end up staring at a screen watching Tic Tok videos 90% of their waking hours.

Chapter 12

"You Incorporated" Part 3-Churning! Wealth Building Bootcamp

Money as a means, not an end

It would be easy to misinterpret the "If money will solve it, it's an expense, not a problem" concept discussed in Chapter 7 as me advocating to not be concerned with money and to "live for the moment...just spend, baby, spend!" As highlighted in the last chapter, nothing could be further from the truth. I strongly believe that you need to manage the financial side of your life *like a business and to spend intentionally.*

The accumulation of money in and of itself doesn't automatically achieve the end game...sustained happiness. To me, there is a balance between building wealth for you and your family's security and using some of that wealth to live the life you want to live while also helping others.

My dad's Florida condo dream

I was blessed with having a dad who always had (and as of this writing, approaching the age of 94, *still* has) a passion for finance and investing. My parents were a couple of those depression era kids that I briefly described earlier in the book...as they grew up, they remained very conservative in how they spent their hard-earned money.

By today's standards, my dad grew up very poor but ultimately was a successful corporate financial officer for a Fortune 500 company for many years, and today lives comfortably. Yet, in my opinion, he is still affected, from a money standpoint, by the poverty he experienced as a youngster growing up around the coal fields and steel mills of western Pennsylvania in the 1930s. I empathize with him: when you live with the type of poverty he had at an early age, you never want to go back to it.

My dad is an expert at investing…it's a passion and he's good at it. Growing up, I learned a lot from him on this topic and we have always enjoyed talking about the market and the economy. I still get valuable insights from him.

I think because my upbringing was relatively easy compared to his, he and I look at money very differently. Money seems to be the end game for my dad: he seems to get more enjoyment from managing the growth of his portfolio than he does from using his wealth to enhance his life. Because he's so "focused on the zeros" in his portfolio, he stresses a lot more than I do on expenses and market corrections can really bother him, even though these will have zero impact on his ability to continue living life the way he wants to.

As an example of this, (and this is a running, good-natured, family joke) my dad looked at buying a vacation home in Florida literally for decades. I am not talking about looking once or twice since he first started his quest in the early 1970s, I am talking about looking virtually every year he and my mom vacationed in Florida during this time period.

I believe my dad's dream of buying a place in Florida was rooted in having a home for the family to spend time together, and as a place for he and my mom to vacation during the cold Ohio winters. When my dad first envisioned this dream, he may not have had the discretionary money to make the purchase. At some point though, he could have swung the investment.

While my dad did not deplete his portfolio by buying that Florida condo, what was the cost of the choice not to buy? Aside from the truly righteous return any waterfront property in Florida would have generated during this multi-decade time frame (that 2 bedroom 2 bath condo on the Gulf coast that he could have bought for $40,000 in the 70's, for $150,000 in the 80's, for $400,000 in the 90's, and now for just a tad over $2.5 million in the current Covid-crazed Florida real estate bubble!), he would have achieved his goal of creating a home where dozens of family vacations probably would have occurred. He would also have had a place that could have been handed down to his kids and grandkids, which might have been worth more than money because of the memories enjoyed there.

Instead, by not buying the condo, today *maybe* he has a higher net worth. Then again, it's very possible his net worth would be higher had he made the purchase, with the likely appreciation that Florida home purchase would have generated.

Money as a tool to enhance your life as well as those around you

This example is not intended to knock my dad…I love him and respect his judgment and I understand the background in which he was raised that created his views about money. Everyone makes their own spending decisions and those should be respected.

I believe the savings and investment discipline my dad exhibits is excellent. Where we differ is that I view money as a means rather than an end in itself. For me, the value of building wealth is to provide security to maintain our standard of living, and ***as importantly***, to use it to live our lives to the fullest as well as to help our sons, church, and other worthy causes we support. I'd rather do these things at the risk of not having as big of a portfolio balance when I die.

This money mindset allows me to not really stress much when the market goes down a lot; as it does from time to time, including now as I complete this book. As explained in these "You Incorporated" chapters, if you have a proper handle on your financial game plan and investments, then you view market drops as an opportunity, and not as the time to lose sleep because your portfolio number on a piece of paper is smaller than it was yesterday…life's too short and precious for that.

You don't need an MBA to successfully build wealth

In this chapter, I'm focusing on the really useful, life-changing basic knowledge of financial management implanted in me by my dad at an early age, and expanded upon later in life by a few grad school professors, including Dr. Joe Morrison and the late Dr. David A. Bowers at the Weatherhead School of Management at Case Western Reserve University in Cleveland. It's my hope these fundamentals will help you achieve financial independence and, more importantly, support *your* path to sustained happiness…all without paying a financial advisor a big hunk of your wealth over the course of your life.

Financial education for most Americans is pretty poor. If you are lucky, your parents will teach you the basics on the importance of savings and maybe you will stumble upon a decent personal economics class in high school. I firmly believe in getting kids started early with understanding basic financial concepts such as money, the cost of goods and services, and making financial choices which, Ta-Da!, results in financial goal setting at an early age. The goal at the age of 5 might be to save enough money for a new Pokemon plushy, and at 10, the goal might be a new video game system. The basic concepts of setting a goal, working to accumulate the money to buy it, and foregoing other choices of spending the money needed to achieve the goal, are the same that adults face every day of their lives.

When my two sons were young, I would give them an allowance each week based on a set of daily chores. They could earn extra money or other privileges (for example, extra screen time) by doing additional chores or other tasks. My kids had **levers** that could influence their "Earning"/income (more or less chores) and their "Burning"/spending (buy candy now or save for the video game later). Their discipline and earning power determined how quickly their goals were achieved.

News Flash! The above childish example also exactly describes your life and mine from a financial standpoint. Easy as it may be to blame society or other outside forces, you control how much you earn in the short and long term. I know that statement seems harsh and does not provide you with much wiggle room in terms of other excuses that explain your current financial predicament…but it's true…you are the CEO of You Incorporated and you determine how much revenue You Incorporated will generate.

How do you "Churn"/invest the dough to make it grow?
From reading the last two chapters, hopefully, you have your arms around how you are going to earn your dough while resisting the urge to burn too much money through budgeting and intentional spending. You now need to think about how you are going to "churn"/ invest that hard earned money to also support your goals.

Over the course of your career, the way you save and invest your earnings can be a more important factor in determining your long term financial wealth and security than your earning power: There are many examples of people who never earned more than an average income, but due to the way they managed their burn and churn levers, they became millionaires nonetheless. So if you want to build wealth, it is important you take ownership of becoming the CFO (Chief Financial Officer) of You Incorporated as well as the CEO (Chief Executive Officer).

Life Hack #28: Take control of your investments! Many people focus the majority of their attention as it relates to building wealth on the "Earning" lever, trying to find ways to make more money through work. While this is important, people frequently relegate the "Churning"/Investing lever to a "financial advisor" because they don't feel comfortable or confident making investment decisions competently on

their own. In my opinion, *this is a huge mistake* and can cost you significant long term wealth in terms of the fees you will pay over the course of your life, as well as the likely subpar returns that advisor (net of all costs) will provide versus what you can earn learning and applying the simple approaches I explain here.

"It's easier to fool people than to convince them they have been fooled"-Mark Twain

"Why not just use an investment advisor? They only charge a few percent to manage my money, right?"

Don't be fooled...that 2% does add up big time over the long run. The following shows the impact on your wealth if you were to pay an investment advisor 2% of your portfolio per year to manage your investments vs the return you would earn in a low cost S&P 500 index fund:

	Invest-age 35	Value-age 65	Difference
S&P 500 Index Fund	$100,000	$1,744,940	
	$250,000	$4,362,508	
	$500,000	$8,724,701	
Investment Advisor*	$100,000	$1,006,266	$(738,674)
	$250,000	$2,515,664	$(1,846,844)
	$500,000	$5,031,328.	$(3,693,373)

*The above assumes no additional savings are contributed after age 35. It also assumes the total incremental cost of the investment advisor compared to the low cost index fund is 2% per year.

This cost could be a bit less or significantly more depending on the loads and other fees associated with the investments the advisor uses in addition to the fee he directly charges you.

This also assumes the advisor is able to match the average 10% gross return (8% after the 2% advisor fee) the S&P 500 has produced over the long term and is assumed to produce here. As the study that follows shows, that's not a given...the advisor will often ***not*** be able to match the index rate of return and the "cost" of using the advisor is often even more than shown above!

Yes, that 2% DOES add up, doesn't it? I don't know about you, but I'd rather have that $738,000-$3,243,373 million riding in my bank account rather than paying for my investment advisor's beach house! Hopefully, you now see why I am so passionate about you learning to manage your investments on your own.

But my local advisor is a financial genius!

I know what you're thinking...especially those of you who *are currently paying* a financial advisor to manage your money. You are thinking your local investment advisor outperforms a basic low cost index fund and that's why they're worth the 2% (or whatever the amount is) you pay them. ***The reality is, a low cost S&P 500 index fund typically outperforms <u>the vast majority of all professional fund managers</u>.*** And when I say professional fund managers these are the best of the best, managing millions or billions in assets, not your local guy who is likely doing even worse.

In fact, there's a study called the SPIVA Scorecard (SPIVA stands for S&P Indices Versus Active) that measures the performance of the S&P 500 vs all professionally managed large cap funds. It's produced every six months. ***The latest report, from June 2021, shows that over the past 20 years, the S&P 500 index outperformed 94.05% of all US active large cap stock fund managers. Make sure you understand that: investing in the S&P 500 index beats over 94% of all professional fund managers' performance over the last 20 years. If they had a SPIVA card measuring the index's performance against small town USA investment advisors, I'm guessing the index would beat 99.99999% of them.***

The bottom line is, in good times or bad, no matter what strategy an active fund manager uses, over time, they just do not outperform the market benchmark S&P 500. You are not only forking over a lot of your money to the personal investment advisor, you are almost guaranteed to have subpar returns on your investments.

Now that I hopefully have your attention...

The intent of this book is to cut through the noise that, frankly, is designed to keep you intimidated as it relates to investing your money yourself. My goal here is to demystify how you can properly invest your hard earned money and earn, over time, a better return after costs are factored in than you can using an advisor, without taking undue risk. Sound good? Sound impossible? It's not, and hopefully, you will find it's doable and you will take control of your financial future for the sake of you and your family.

There is a multi-trillion dollar industry out there that is set up with the intent, for the most part, to make you, the average person, think you need someone else to make intelligent decisions about how to invest your money. **This is a lie.**

It blows me away how many smart, experienced professional people I know that turn one of the most important responsibilities they have as an adult, their wealth building, over to some local financial advisor. They pay their advisors big dollars every year to invest their money, generally, with no better and typically worse returns than if they had invested their money on their own, without most of the fees.

When I hear guys talking about how they "just met with their financial advisor to talk about investing strategy," I'm not impressed that this guy has a financial advisor. Instead, I'm usually feeling sorry for them because I know (as the cost analysis and SPIVA data shows), in all likelihood, they are paying a significant chunk of change for the pleasure of having their advisor produce sub-par returns, especially when costs are factored in.

I wonder if they use an advisor because they don't know where to get the basic skills to manage their own money, or if they somehow think being at a point in their life where they can afford a financial advisor is some sort of status symbol, or if they simply lack the courage to take on the important responsibility of managing their wealth. No matter the reason, in my opinion, it's a bad choice that will most likely result in *having significantly less* wealth in the future rather than more.

Concepts and tools to show how you can outperform most pros

This book is not intended to explain all there is to know about the world of finance. It's intended to show you, in a simple, straightforward way, how you can take control of your financial life by establishing sound savings habits and by making prudent investments to grow wealth over the long term successfully, with minimal risk and cost.

While it's true there are an almost infinite number of ways to invest your money, some of which are extremely complicated, I am here to tell you that, over the long run, you yourself can achieve, through the use of low cost index funds, investment performance as good or better than most professional money managers.

This section will lay out in simple language how you can effectively manage your money yourself and how you can adjust your investments during the course of your life as new financial goals arise. I will also point out a handful of really useful resources you can access to learn more about personal investing...none of which require an MBA or even a college degree to understand.

Let's start with the basics: investment asset classes

There are a couple of key concepts and terms you need to clearly understand before becoming the CFO of You Inc. The first concept is the "asset classes" of investments. These include equities, bonds, cash, and real estate as well as a newer entrant to the party, cryptocurrencies, that you've probably heard a lot about.

Equities is a fancy name for shares of stock in publicly traded companies. Historically, equities provide by far the highest average return on each dollar you invest…roughly 10% per year before inflation over the past 100 or so years.

When you buy stock in a company, you are buying a piece of the ownership of that company. When you own stock, you are entitled to receive regular financial reports from the company (easily accessible online) and to vote on key issues facing the company from time to time.

There are two basic ways you can make money on a stock:

- The primary way is that, over time, the company generates a growing income stream and as a result, the value/price of the stock goes up.

- A second way you can earn money on stocks is that some companies pay dividends. Essentially, the dividend is a way of sharing some of the earned profits from the company with each shareholder.

Typically, slower growth companies pay a dividend while faster growing companies prefer to reinvest all of their earnings in the business to maximize their growth potential which should translate into a higher share price over the long run.

To do a proper job in picking individual stocks to buy, I'm old school in believing you need to thoroughly research the company and understand what makes it tick, and why it would be a good investment over the long term. There are many people today who just follow the news and bet on a hot stock that appears to be a good buy without any real knowledge of the company: I call this gambling, not investing, and I strongly advise against it.

Index funds are the way regular investors beat most pros

So what's a regular person, who doesn't have the time or inclination to research hundreds of companies, supposed to do in order to capture the superior return stocks historically provide? The answer, as you have likely guessed from the SPIVA data, is to consider investing in index mutual funds or ETFs (exchange traded funds). Index funds hold large baskets of individual stock. The S&P 500 Index fund, for example, holds shares of stock for all 500 companies in the S&P 500.

When I was working on my MBA in the mid-80's, the first index mutual fund had just been introduced a few years earlier by Vanguard. One of the real nuggets I got from my MBA experience was in Professor Joe Morrison's Investment Portfolio Finance class, where he highlighted how this new class of investments…index mutual funds…was actually beating more than 70% of professionally managed stock pickers' results every year…and at a fraction of the cost of trading individual stocks through a broker. I jumped on this knowledge and have been investing in index funds, including the original Vanguard S&P 500 Index Fund, ever since.

While it is exciting to get lucky and pick a hot stock, for new and average investors, the far better and more secure way to invest in equities is to regularly invest in an index fund. In fact, even though I've been successfully investing in stocks since I was a teenager, today, most of my portfolio is in index funds. More about how index funds work later.

Bonds are another class of investments. Bonds are loan obligations of public or private entities. The US government, for example, issues a variety of treasury bonds for funding its ever-growing spending. Companies also sell bonds to help finance their growth plans.

Both bonds and equities are used by companies to raise money for their business. The difference is that bonds are essentially a loan and typically generate an interest payment. At the end of the bond term (called the bond's maturity), the investor also gets paid back the original principal of the bond.

With stocks, you become an owner of the company. With bonds, you become a lender to the company. Because of this distinction stocks are inherently more risky than bonds and, on average, they generate a higher return to attract investors to this higher risk.

Bonds do have risk though and, like stocks, the value of a particular bond can go up and down in value based on the risk of that particular bond (while US government bonds are considered "risk free," an individual company's bonds would likely drop in value if there is risk the company may go bankrupt, for example). Bond values also generally move in the opposite direction of interest rate changes…a prime example is in early 2022, bond values have been falling as the government started raising interest rates in an effort to slow down raging inflation.

Like a mortgage you get on your house, bonds can have different terms. Some bonds or "notes" from the US treasury have terms of only a few months. Other bonds from both companies and governments can extend many years and even decades. The longer the life/term of the bond, the more its value will be affected (up or down) by interest rate changes.

Cash is a third asset class. Cash means readily accessible money in either a bank, a money market account, or under your mattress. When I was young, bank savings accounts paid about 5% interest. Not so today. As of this writing, the best savings accounts pay only about 0.55% interest (I use Barclay's Online Savings account to park most of my cash).

Most bank and money market accounts are federally insured up to $250,000 so, essentially, they are "risk free." Because they are risk free, investors don't require or get much of a return on their money. Despite the low return, when the world is going crazy, as it is in early 2022, sometimes it's best to park some of your money in cash and ride out the storm vs bonds.

Real Estate is a fourth asset class. This includes the equity you have in your home or investment properties you might own. You can also invest in real estate through an investment type called a REIT..a real estate investment trust…where someone else manages a group of properties but as an investor, you own a share of the properties and receive a share in the profits/returns.

Cryptocurrency. Since the introduction of Bitcoin in 2008, a broad array of different cryptocurrencies has been introduced into the marketplace. A core objective of the underlying technology that powers these, called blockchains, is to ensure all transactions are transparent, traceable, and that the system is hacker proof, all without the need for a middleman like a government or a bank.

Blockchains are truly revolutionary and, beyond bitcoin, there are some remarkable crypto innovations, like smart contracts and NFTs (non fungible tokens). These have the potential to disrupt and remake a lot of the traditional business landscape. That being said, these assets are highly risky and volatile. I've included a chapter providing more details on the interesting world of cryptocurrencies later in the book.

Because the focus of this discussion is to help folks do the basics, from an investing standpoint, and to securely build wealth over time, I do not suggest that folks who are at this stage of their financial journey dabble in any cryptocurrencies, just as I would not suggest betting on individual stocks or to trade options. There is significant money to be made in all these types of investments to be sure but, again, the focus here is to provide the basics of building a solid, proven, and sustainable investment strategy to grow your wealth without the need for an expensive outside advisor.

Each asset class has a role to play

The above asset classes have unique characteristics in terms of risk and reward. From an historical perspective, excluding cryptos, equities produce the highest average annual returns. Equities also have the greatest volatility. Volatility means there is greater potential for dramatic (up or down) changes in value over the short and sometimes intermediate term. So while equities might, over a 100 year period, on average, generate a 10% annual return, there are periods, including early 2022, when there have been significant double digit declines in value. There were intermediate periods of several years when equity returns have been flat or only slightly positive. Bonds, on the other hand, produce lower long term average returns but are generally much less volatile. Cash is much less volatile than bonds.

Asset ownership

There are also different ways you can own these various asset classes, which I briefly describe below:

Direct ownership-this means you directly own the asset. For example, when you purchase shares of a company's stock or bond through a broker, or when you buy a rental property as a real estate investment.

Mutual Funds-Both mutual funds and ETFs (described below) hold baskets of stocks, bonds, even real estate, as well as hard assets like gold, and in the not too distant future, cryptocurrencies. Some mutual funds focus on humans making individual investment decisions such as which stocks or bonds to buy and hold. Other mutual funds, known as index funds (described in more detail below), use computers and seek to track a particular index, such as the S&P 500 (the stocks of the 500 largest US public companies). When you buy or sell a mutual fund, the transaction price for that buy or sell is determined at the close of that trading day.

Exchange Traded Funds (ETFs)-ETFs share most of the same characteristics as mutual funds with one important difference: ETFs can be traded in real time during the course of a trading day whereas mutual funds, as noted above, get transacted at the close of each trading day. For a basic investor who is not trading a lot this is not that important, but for an active trader, the use of ETFs allows you to get into and out of an investment at a desired price vs relying on what that investment's price is at the close of business.

Life Hack #29: To take control of your investments, you MUST learn the basics of asset classes and types of investments in order to manage your financial affairs and successfully build wealth over time. Read the above sections until they make sense and, if needed find additional, more detailed free information and descriptions of these concepts online at Vanguard, Fidelity, Schwab, or any other consumer-focused investment company.

Nuts and bolts...

Now that you have an understanding of the types of asset classes, let's cover a few concepts you need to think about related to building wealth before we get into how you can invest for success.

Risk & reward: A basic concept in investing is the more risk a given investment entails, the more reward you should require as an investor to take a chance on that investment. As I described above, equities (stock in individual companies) have more inherent risk generally than bonds, and both of these asset classes have much more risk than cash.

Because of the higher risk, over the past 100 or so years, equities have generated, on average, a 10% (before inflation) annual return on investment. Since 1928, for example, the S&P 500 index, which is a good benchmark for the performance of the US stock market, has declined by as much as 43.8% (in 1931) and increased by as much as 52.6% in 1954. During this time period, there were 63 (out of a total of 92) years where the annual percentage increases or decreases in the index was more than 10%...that's pretty volatile!

Bonds, on average during that same time period, have generated a 3% (before inflation) return on investment. US Treasury bonds increased in value by as much as plus 32.8% (in 1982) and declined by as much as minus 11.1% (in 2009) in a given year during that time period. However, there were only 20 years (out of a total of 92) where the annual change in value was greater than 10%...still some volatility, but you can see much less than with stocks.

A word about cash!

Some folks consider cash "risk free." That may be true in the very short term if you put your money in a savings account that the FDIC insures up to $250,000 per account. The balance you hold in that account won't go up or down on a daily basis, other than for the paltry interest banks now pay.

However, over the long term, there is risk that relates to the devaluation of the dollar as the US government prints ever more prodigious quantities of currency. Since 2020, the money supply (called "M2" by economists) has grown from less than $16 trillion to $21.2 trillion, or more than 34%, without any corresponding increase in the value the US economy has generated. While the dollar you hold in your hand still looks and feels like a dollar, the reality is it's worth, frighteningly enough, is only about $.66 compared to the same dollar you held in your hand in early 2020. You can see this in the inflation of goods and services you buy: the house that cost $100k in 2020 now easily costs $120-130k. Same with used cars and many other assets, even daily consumables like gas and food.

The truth is, the longer the period of time you hold cash in bank and money market accounts, the less those dollars are worth when you go to spend them in terms of the actual goods they will buy. That's why smart investors invest in real assets during times of inflation (caused almost always, including now, by the government printing too much money).

Real assets include real estate, gold, collectible cars, art, and stocks, which represent companies that have plants and inventory.

The growing concerns of the US devaluing its currency by printing too much money have also been a key driver for people looking at alternatives like Bitcoin, which has a fixed supply.

When you make any investment decision, you are really weighing the risk/reward tradeoff; trying to strike a balance to earn a reasonable return on your money for the amount of risk you are taking. The longer your time horizon for when you need to spend the money, the more risk you can afford to take in order to earn a higher return.

What is your risk tolerance?

There are two sides to risk tolerance. The first is how you personally handle risk as it relates to your finances. The second relates more to how much risk conventional wisdom says you should be taking at a given point in your wealth-building journey. I'll call this second type of risk "life stage" risk.

Your personal risk tolerance

Some people are intrinsically risk-averse when it comes to money. Others have a wild gambler mentality. My view is some level of balance is usually the best approach for most things in life and investing is no exception.

- If you take no risk and put your money in "risk free" assets like a savings account or even Treasury bonds, your wealth will erode over time due to inflation and the government printing more dollars. For example, if inflation is at 3% and you are earning 0.5% in a "high yield" savings account, your wealth after inflation is shrinking…you have negative "Churn" of 2.4% per year. That's no way to become a millionaire.

- Conversely, if you are always betting on the next hot stock or trying to time the market, jumping in and out of your investments frequently, or randomly throwing your investment dollars around in a disorganized way, there are high odds you will frequently find yourself going backwards in the long term, if not going all the way back to zero at some point. That's also no way to become a millionaire.

The bottom line is, in order to build wealth over the long term, you need to be able to deal with some level of risk in your investments, and be secure in the knowledge that history indicates, over the long term, that this is the correct investing strategy.

Understanding your risk tolerance is important because the long term goal is sustained happiness and it's hard to be happy if you are constantly worried about your investments changing in value every day (which they will). Having the underlying knowledge of how different investments perform will hopefully arm you with the confidence to accept reasonable levels of risk and volatility in your investments so you can effectively grow your wealth.

Life stage risk-specific purchases

There is another important type of risk that comes into play at various stages of your life. For example, if you are planning to buy a house in the next two years, would it be smart to have your downpayment for that house all invested in the stock market, knowing, from the historical information noted previously there is a chance it could decline in a given year by 40%? No, that would not be a smart move.

This is a good example of life stage risk. My advice to my kids is that if you really need to spend the money in the next 3 years, don't have that money invested in equities or bonds or cryptos for that matter. Have that downpayment money in a secure, low risk (and yes, low return) bank or money market account.

This is an example of adjusting your investments for important things that occur at various stages in your life. It doesn't mean you divert all your savings away from your long term wealth building plan… just the portion of your savings that relates to saving for your house downpayment, in this example.

Life stage risk-as you get older

There is a second type of life stage risk, which relates to adjusting your investing strategy over the course of your life. Conventional financial wisdom would say the earlier you are in your life, the more investment risk you should take because, as shown above, over the long term, certain investment types such as equities, always outperform other investment types, like cash or bonds. This is the whole theory behind newer "target retirement" mutual funds that adjust the investment ratio between equities and bonds as you get closer to a target retirement date.

For example, in your 20's, a target fund might hold 90% of your investment in equities and 10% in bonds. As you get closer to retirement, the percent might change to 60% equities and 40% bonds, in order to de-risk your portfolio.

While there is much debate on what the exact right % mix of equities vs. bonds should be at a given point in your life, the above example is probably not too far off the mark. The younger you are, the larger % of your wealth should be invested in higher risk/higher return asset types such as equities. The closer you are to needing to spend that money in retirement, you want the higher percentage to be in lower risk assets like cash and bonds that will be available to spend when you need it to supplement or replace your earned income. I will provide some investment approaches to consider in the next chapter.

Portfolio allocation

Ok, now this sounds really sophisticated doesn't it? What the hell is a "portfolio"? And what do you know about "allocating" it? All this means is how much of your total investable wealth (your portfolio) is allocated to each of the asset classes I described above. As noted, if you need a specific chunk of money in the next few years to make a downpayment on a house or to buy a car, you want to allocate that portion of your portfolio to a secure, low risk and low return (unfortunately) asset class like cash. You don't want a major market correction to happen and wipe out your house downpayment in the blink of an eye.

On the flip side, when you have a 2 year old and are saving for his or her college or when you are saving for retirement, with these longer time horizons, you want to allocate more of your portfolio into riskier/higher returning assets like stocks. These choices are what portfolio allocation means.

Dollar cost averaging

"The stock market is a device to transfer money from the impatient to the patient"-Warren Buffett

Once you implement the budget process suggested in the prior chapter, and the extra dollars start flowing in each month after expenses, it's really gratifying to know you and your spouse are in control of your financial destiny, and this builds confidence to keep doing it.

The next step is to set up an automatic method to save and invest those extra dollars. This has two benefits: first, by having money automatically taken out of your paycheck and/or checking account each pay period or month, it makes those dollars less likely to be spent. The best way is to set up payroll deductions, that way the money never even hits your checking account and you mentally adapt to not having those extra dollars, potentially tempting you to spend them.

The second benefit, (and this is a really important concept in investing) is called dollar cost averaging. Dollar cost averaging simply means making regularly timed investments in a given asset, such as an index fund.

Many places of work offer tax deferred savings plans. These are known as 401ks if you work for a private company, and 403bs if you work for a government or non-profit entity. These plans encourage workers to contribute as a way of building wealth for retirement.

I'll get into the benefits of these types of plans in the next chapter. But for now, as an example, let's say you are just starting out of college in your early 20's and your company's 401k plan is set up with Vanguard, a well established investment company that I've personally used my entire working life. In your company's 401k plan, you have multiple investment options but for this example, let's assume you decide to invest your monthly contribution in Vanguard's Target Retirement 2065 mutual fund. This plan automatically adjusts the allocation weight of stocks and bonds as you age, becoming more conservative (and weighted towards bonds) as you get closer to retirement, in this case with a target retirement year of 2065.

Putting your budgeted savings to work

- After doing your budget, you decide you want to save 10% of your $3,000 monthly income, or $300 each month.

- Further, you decide half of this $300 (or $150) will go into your 401k contribution and into the Vanguard Target Retirement 2065 fund as an automatic deduction from your paycheck.

- The other half ($150) will go into a separate non-401k investment account you will manage on your own as an automatic deduction out of your checking account each month.

- In your budget, you treat these investments like savings and account for them as such. Many financial advisors call this "paying yourself first" and it's a good concept to help ensure that savings is a regular part of your monthly expenditures, just like food and electricity.

- Once you have made these elections and set up the automatic payroll and checking account deductions, you are on autopilot and dollar cost averaging comes into play: the money from your paycheck automatically gets invested into your selected investment every time you get paid, and the money being invested out of your checking account occurs on the same day each month in which you select.

By doing these investments on the same days each month, you are assured of not always buying at the highest or lowest point in the market, and over time you are assured of buying at some average dollar amount. This helps ensure you secure the return that the underlying market you are investing in is pretty close to the average, which is what you are seeking to do.

Many people go through life randomly investing money when they hear the stock market is hot and then pulling their money out of the market when they get spooked their investment is going down in value when the market is falling. **This approach to investing is guaranteed to make you a loser over the long run!** Professional fund managers make the same mistake, trying to time the market. This is one of the primary reasons both individual and professional investors do not perform as well as an index fund.

By dollar cost averaging your money into either a target fund or specific index funds and ***leaving that money in the investments you select over the course of your career,*** you will ensure by not bouncing in and out of the market that you *will* get returns which closely match the market index (for example, the S&P 500 if you invest in a fund that tracks that index).

Given the market, historically, always goes up in the long term, you are guaranteed to grow your wealth over the long term. It's as simple as that. This is disciplined investing guaranteed to grow your wealth significantly over the long run without paying all that extra cash for an advisor.

Life Hack #30: Armed with a clear understanding of these basic concepts, you will be able to competently manage your assets and make informed decisions on how to allocate your investments as you go through your career

and life. Automatic investing and dollar cost averaging your investments are key elements in building your wealth over the long term by removing the need, or temptation, for you to randomly jump in and out of investments yourself.

Interested in seeing how rich you can be? Use the rule of 72s

The rule of 72s sounds like some mystic incantation but it's really a very simple way to assess the growth or cost of different investment/ purchase decisions. This is such an important concept. I tried to make sure my sons understood this at an early age...around 14 or 15.

Here's how it works: If you make an assumption on the annual rate of return on an investment and divide that assumed rate of return into the number 72, the result will tell you how many years it will take to double your money.

- For example, let's assume you have an investment in a mutual fund that matches the performance of the US stock market. There are many such investments available, which I'll discuss later, but to determine the expected return on investment, you could use the actual ~100 year average annual return the US stock market has produced before inflation of about 10%.

- To use the rule of 72s, you take that 10% expected annual rate of return and divide it into 72. The result is 7.2. That means if you invest in a fund that matches the US stock market, and that fund performs in a similar way as it has for the past 100 years, and you earn 10% on average annually, your money in that fund will double roughly every 7.2 years.

- Expected rate of return/72= years it will take for your money to double.

The power of the rule of 72s: you can use this to plan retirement as well as to evaluate the impact of major expenses on building wealth.

Rule of 72s in action!

- Let's say you are 23 years old and have been diligently saving your hard earned dough as well as the gifts you received from your high school and college graduations.
- You now have $35,000 invested in an index mutual fund that matches the S&P 500.
- You know, from applying the rule of 72s and the example above, that money is likely to earn on average 10% and double roughly every 7 years.
- Now you want to know, what will the value of your $35,000 be if you just leave it alone and never save or withdraw a single dime until you retire at age 65?

It's simple!

1. You calculate your expected years to retirement. In the above example, we'll assume that is 65 years minus your current age of 23. That equals 42 years until retirement.
2. You now divide 42 by the rule of 72s number of years to double your money, which we showed is 7.
3. The 42 years until retirement divided by 7 is 6. This means that the $35,000 you currently have in this investment will double 6 times by the time you retire at age 65.
4. Let's do the fun math here:
    1. The first doubling turns your $35k into $70k.
    2. The second doubling makes it $140k.
    3. The third doubling makes it $280k.
    4. The fourth doubling makes it $560k.

5. The fifth doubling makes it $1.12 million
6. And the sixth and final doubling makes it $2.24 million!

H*oly cow, if you were smart and hard working enough to have saved $35k by age 22 and invested it as noted, you'd be a multi-millionaire by age 65, <u>without ever contributing another dollar to that investment account over the rest of your life.</u> That's some real dough!*

Imagine how your wealth would grow even more dramatically if you continued to dollar cost average investments into that fund for the rest of your career...like magic, you'd be guaranteed of being a millionaire many times over at retirement (assuming future market returns are similar over the long run to past returns)!

Truth be told, the above is exactly what I've done. I started putting money from every paycheck into Vanguard's Index 500 when I first started working out of college. And while my investments have become more complex and diverse over the past ~35 years, that discipline and those good habits have built the portfolio I have today.

I've never used an investment advisor of any sort and I've never pulled money out of the market during the several crashes I've lived through...including the current one unfolding in early 2022. To the contrary, more often than not, I've invested ***more*** money into the market when it tanks and everyone else is selling and saying the "sky is falling." Is it sometimes nerve wracking to see your portfolio dive by 30-40%, like it did in the 2008-2009 crash? Yes, it can be, but over time you trust the US economy will bounce back, often in spite of the idiots that run our government.

"Most people get interested in stocks when everyone else is. The time to get interested is when no one else is. You can't buy what is popular and do well."-Warren Buffett

Building wealth over time is really that simple if you master the concepts above. You don't have to pay an investment advisor a few percent of your wealth every year to invest your money.

The rule of 72s in reverse

Here's a sad but too often true flip-side example of using the rule of 72s to assess the impact on your future wealth based on a "Burning"/ spending decision:

- Let's assume the same scenario as noted above, but instead of putting that $35k you saved into a S&P 500 index fund and letting it ride for the next 42 years, you decide to splurge and spend that money on a new boat to use at the lake on weekends and impress all your friends.
- While the boat is costing you $35k in today's dollars, it's really costing you over $2.24 million in potential future retirement dollars because that $35k won't be growing and multiplying over the next 42 years like the index fund will! Kind of an eye opener, isn't it?

Hopefully, you can see how having this simple tool in your bag of tricks might allow you to make wiser investment and spending decisions. Again, all you need to use the rule of 72s is to have an estimated annual return amount and an estimate of how many years you will let the money grow.

Life Hack #31: The rule of 72s is one of the simplest yet most powerful tools to assess the future potential impact of spending and investing decisions due to the magic of compounding. Using this tool can help you project, based on your current savings and investing approach and by making an estimate on your future return on investment, how much money you can reasonably expect to have at some point in the future. This can help you determine for example, when you can afford to retire.

Life Hack #32: To get the benefits of compounding and the rule of 72s and to have a good shot at building significant

wealth over your lifetime:

- **You need to let the money you invest ride! Do not pull it in and out of the market when the market goes up and down because you or some friend has an insight the market will crash or the economy will take a dump. Suck it up and ride these bumps out.**
- **Keep dollar cost averaging your money into low cost, diversified index funds or ETFs and let it grow.**

Diversification

Another key concept to understand is diversification. What this concept holds is that you can lower your risk but maintain returns on your overall investments by diversifying or spreading where your money is invested.

My intention is to keep this fairly simple so I won't get into the empirical analysis to prove this concept but take my word for it or, better yet, Duck Duck Go the topic for more detailed information. If you spread your investment dollars, over multiple companies in a given type of market (say US public companies), your risk is much less than if you simply pick one US company and buy their stock. Over the long term, your return on investment should not be meaningfully hurt by this diversification.

When I was young, trading stocks was quite expensive (on the order of $100 in broker fees to buy 100 shares of stock) and index mutual funds did not exist until the mid-70's. As a result, at that time, diversification for an individual investor was not very practical: your returns would have been hammered by the transaction costs needed to buy several different stocks, let alone buying the entire S&P 500.

Today, the world is different and almost anyone can invest in a wide range of highly diversified portfolios very inexpensively. Index mutual funds and ETFs are ideal investment vehicles to achieve diversification, and I will describe some of these later.

What's better, in recent years, some of the larger fund companies like Vanguard and Fidelity have reduced or eliminated many of their investment fees and the required investment to set up an account at these companies is typically only a few thousand dollars. Both of these companies, as well as many others, offer a broad range of fairly easy to understand information on investing and describe each of their funds' investment goals which is perfect for you, as a new investor, to increase your knowledge (see the reference section for their website links).

Life Hack #33-Diversification: spread your risk while maintaining your return by diversifying your investments rather than picking individual stocks and, in the long run, you will be better off. The easiest and most cost-effective way to do this is by investing in an index (see below) mutual fund or ETF that seeks to match the performance of a specific market such as the S&P 500.

Indexing

What is indexing? All this means is that you are buying a type of investment that has the objective to mirror the performance...both the ups and downs...of a particular market index.

The first index mutual fund, introduced in 1975 by Jack Bogle's Vanguard Group, was designed to match the performance of the S&P 500, a group of 500 US "blue chip" stocks. It does this by simply buying and owning all 500 of these stocks in proportion to their individual stock values. Why is tracking the S&P 500 desirable? Well, since 1926, before the depression and in spite of many market collapses since then, year in and year out over that long time period, the S&P 500 has produced an average annual return of 10.1%.

As you now know from reading about the rule of 72s, that means your money, on average over the long term, doubles about every 7 years (72 divided by 10.1 = 7.13 years). Even better, over the past 10 years, the return has been 14.8% doubling every 4.9 years! That means if you had $1 million dollars invested in this fund 10 years ago, and didn't add another dollar to it - just let it grow, it would have doubled twice and you would now have $4 million in less than 10 years today. That, my friend, is the simple, fool-proof way to build wealth, and all without paying an advisor!

An S&P 500 index fund almost exactly (within hundredths of a percent) matches the actual performance of these 500 individual stocks so you get what you pay for: essentially you are betting on the ongoing, long term strength of the US economy as reflected in its 500 largest public companies. Is that performance better than you, financial genius that you are or the local investment advisor you might be paying to invest your money can produce? As shown in the latest SPIVA scorecard shown earlier, yes, it's better than 94% of all professional fund managers over the past 20 years.

To quote Warren Buffet, one of the world's richest men and arguably the world's premier stock investor one last time:

"Huge institutional investors, viewed as a group, have long underperformed the unsophisticated index-fund investor who simply sits tight for decades."

Bottom line: while not sexy or exciting, indexing works and is the best way, short of relying on luck, for you to produce returns that match the performance of the overall market over the long run. It allows you, the little guy, to generate investment returns that are better than the vast majority of professionally managed portfolios over the long term for very little cost.

Today, there are a myriad of indexing options for both mutual funds and ETFs. You can select bond index funds of various stripes as well as equity/stock index funds for almost any desired investing strategy. Still, it's hard to beat the original S&P 500 index from Vanguard, Fidelity, or other companies who now offer this investment option. That's why, together, the Vanguard and Fidelity 500 Index funds have almost $750 billion invested in them.

Market timing…don't do it!

Among the many mistakes people make when investing their money, trying to "time the market" is one of the biggest. There's lots of empirical data on this but here's reality smacked upside your head: you don't know more than the rest of the financial world, and neither does your investment advisor, about when to buy into or get out of the market. The reality is that each year most major increases in the market as well as most major decreases happen in a tiny handful of days. You are never going to be able to pick any of those days in advance on a consistent basis. Your returns get killed when you miss even one or two major upticks in the market for a given year. **That is why the best way to invest is to dollar cost average your money into your selected investments and then DO NOT TOUCH THEM! <u>JUST LET THEM RIDE!</u>**

Yes, there will be market booms and busts. As discussed above, by buying into the market regularly and leaving your money invested, you will never be caught buying or selling at the worst time. Yes, you also won't buy and sell at the best time either but, as noted previously, won't you feel pretty good about beating, year-in and year-out, more than 90% of the Ivy League eggheads' professionally managed funds, who, in all likelihood, are pulling money in and out of the market needlessly, hurting long term returns? **This isn't a game…it's the serious business of building *your* family's wealth. Do it smartly and don't get sucked into an emotional investment roller coaster.**

Costs matter…duh

Rather than relying on your own brains and the little bit of simple wisdom I am providing in this book, if you decide instead to go to an investment advisor you will pay lots of money over your life for what will likely turn out to be sub-par performance vs average market performance. There are several different fee structures that financial advisors charge their clients. Most advisors either charge a percentage of your portfolio value or a fixed annual fee. For example, if you are a professional and have a portfolio worth $1 million to manage, the annual fee might be 1-2% of your portfolio. Smaller portfolios would typically have a higher percentage charge.

If that weren't bad enough, advisors often times steer you into expensive investment options such as mutual funds with high "loads" or fees in their own right. Advisors often make added commission by putting your money into these high load funds...a pretty cozy little deal if you ask me!

Here's an example of one of these high load funds from 2018:

- American Growth Fund Series One, charges an upfront fee of 2.19% (yes, you pay them upfront to take your money; and a nice chunk of that might get kicked back to your investment advisor).

- In addition, the annual expenses to run that fund are 7.65% every year.

- What do you get for such a platinum-costing mutual fund? Over the prior 10 years, this fund generated a return after expenses of 10.48%, which doesn't sound too bad on the surface.

- However an S&P 500 index fund generated a 14.8% return during this time period and kicked this fund's ass (pardon my French) by 37%. But rest assured, the investment advisor who recommends this fund to his poor clients is happy as he's likely been taking all the fees and commissions his clients have been so graciously paying him, and using it to expand his beachfront estate in Florida.

Here's the icing on the cake for index investors...because these funds are managed by computer and not expensive human stock pickers, their costs are infinitesimal. As of April 2021, the Vanguard 500 Index Fund has an annual expense ratio of 0.04%...yes that's not a typo…it's 4/100's of 1%! For an investment of $10,000, it costs you $4 annually for Vanguard to manage it for you. Compare that to the American Growth fund noted above, where you are paying $985 upfront in year 1 and $765 every year thereafter for their fund managers to get fat as they grossly underperform the market.

Hopefully, I've made my point…sticking with low cost index funds or ETFs puts a lot more money in **your** pocket, not someone else's. All these costs really add up. As shown in the earlier example, these added fees can cost you hundreds of thousands if not millions of dollars over your working career. **Remember-What matters is your net investment return *after* all investment expenses have been subtracted.**

Life Hack #34: Smart investing for everyone. If you are serious about building wealth for yourself and your family, read the above sections until they make sense…these few basic concepts are really all you need to do a proper job of efficiently managing your investments and building your wealth over time without paying someone else to do it for you:

- **Set up your paycheck and your checking account to automatically invest money each pay period or month into your selected investments.**
- **Strongly consider index funds that match your investment goals.**
- **Then leave the money alone so it can breed and multiply!**
- **While you will certainly have some down years, on average, if you stick to these concepts and apply them consistently over your life, you will earn close to the market returns which, as discussed, is better than the vast majority of professional investment advisors.**

Chapter 13

"You Incorporated" Part 4-Getting Started,

Putting Your Money to Work!

In this chapter, I will provide some examples of broadly diversified, low cost index funds that can accomplish the market-matching performance concepts described earlier in the book. Before getting into these investment options, I'll outline a few things you should consider in terms of prioritizing your savings once they start to accumulate.

Step 1-Pay off all your credit cards!

According to data from Finbold, consumer debt in the US topped $14.6 trillion as of Q1, 2021, up a whopping $1 trillion from 2020. That works out to $44,000 per person. While a big chunk of that debt reflects people's mortgages, over $2.3 trillion is tied up in auto and credit card debt. According to WalletHub, in 2021, the average household's credit card balance was $8,006.

Credit card debt is a hole that can be hard to dig out of and can prevent you from ever building meaningful wealth. It makes no sense to invest your money elsewhere if you are paying +18% interest on your credit card debt.

Because of the very high interest rates on this debt, it is critical that once you have your budget in place, ***you pay off this debt as quickly as possible.*** At the same time, get in the life-long habit of paying your bills in full each month. Dave Ramsey is an inspiring evangelist on the critical importance of paying off your debts; I've listed his website in the reference section for more information on this topic.

Step 2-Establish an emergency fund.

It's smart to have an emergency fund. The purpose of this fund is to cover your normal expenses should calamity strike such as you and/or your spouse losing your jobs or encountering some other major expense…a car needing major repair, etc.

The size of this fund is based on your circumstances and your budget. Typically, it's a good habit to have at least 3-6 months of your average monthly expenses saved in an emergency fund. For example, if your budgeted monthly expenses are $3,000, you should have $9,000-18,000 socked away in your emergency fund.

Because you would need this money on short notice, you would only invest the emergency fund in an ultra safe investment such as a savings or money market account, and never in the stock or bond market. After you pay off your credit card debt, getting your emergency fund in place should always be your top priority before making any other investments.

Step 3-Assess your future major expenditures.

Are you saving to buy a car or your first house in the next few years? If so, as noted earlier, it is highly risky to have those funds you are working to accumulate invested in the stock or bond market. My rule of thumb is, if you plan to spend the money in the next 2-3 years, keep that money in a savings or money market account, not in a riskier asset class like stocks or bonds.

Step 4-Does your employer provide a 401k/403b match?

This is low hanging fruit and essentially free money. So, as a rule, the first money you allocate for investment, in my opinion, is that amount which at least maximizes the free money you and your spouse's employers will give you.

As an example, the last company I worked for would match 75% of my 401k contributions up to 6% of my pay. In other words, if I contributed 6% to my 401k, my company would kick in another

4.5% of my pay into the account.

As a simple example, if you are making $100,000 per year, that's $4,500 in free money the company is giving you each year to invest, so you want to make sure you at least contribute enough into your 401k to secure that maximum amount of free money your employer will match.

In addition, assuming you and your spouse select conventional 401k/403b plans (vs a Roth version of these plans), the amount you contribute is tax deferred (meaning you don't pay tax on that amount now...you pay the tax when you take the money out when you retire).

When you add the company match and the tax deferral advantages, the 401k (or 403b) puts a big bang into your savings and wealth building.

Free money from your boss and Uncle Sam

- As an example, let's say your company offers a similar match to the one I highlighted above.
- Again, let's assume you earn $100k per year for simple math:
    - You contribute 6% or $6k during the year out of your pay.
    - Your company matches 75% of that or $4.5k for the year.
    - In total, you saved $10.5k.
    - Because you are putting this combined $10.5k into a 401k, you don't pay any taxes now.
    - Assuming you invest this money in a US stock market index fund, as described in earlier chapters, your money will double approximately every 7 years until you retire, based on past market performance.

- Compare this to what you would have left over if you did not contribute into the 401k and instead invested the same amount in a regular taxable investment account:
    - Instead of $10.5k, you would lose the $4.5k company match and only have the after-tax remnants of the $6k you contributed in a regular investment account.
    - Assuming at this income level, you are in the 22% federal tax bracket, you would have $4,680 to invest, which is the leftover amount from your $6k after taxes.

Would you rather have $10.5k compounding tax deferred until you retire or have $4.68k invested, where you pay tax on whatever that amount earns every year in the future? Hopefully, you can see why it's so important to utilize this approach for the first money you invest.

According to the U.S. Bureau of Labor statistics, in 2018, only 69% of those who have the ability to contribute to a 401k at their place of work do so. That means 31% don't!

It's crazy how many people don't take advantage of their company match and forgo a really awesome, easy way to help build wealth. Also, keep in mind, while it's really important to contribute enough to max-out the employer match, you can contribute much more to a 401k (403b) each year and still derive the tax deferral benefits, which are important over the long-run. For 2022, the maximum you can contribute (not including any employer matching contributions) is $20,500. If you are 50 years old or older, you can contribute an additional $6,500 per year or $27,000 total.

Step 5: Do you have the option of contributing to a Health Savings Account (HSA)?

For many folks, another wonderful piece of low-hanging fruit that is there for the taking is the HSA.

To be eligible for an HSA, you need to participate in a "high deductible health plan (HDHP)" as defined by the IRS. Your employer will highlight this insurance option during your annual benefits enrollment period towards the end of the year.

What's so special about an HSA? It's the only way, that I know of, to invest in a totally tax free way: the amount you contribute is tax deductible, the earnings your HSA accrues are tax free, and when you withdraw money from your HSA and spend it on designated healthcare costs, the funds are also not taxed.

In addition, like the 401k employer match, there is often an employer "kicker" contribution that is totally free to you, the employee. Employers are motivated for their employees to select these high deductible plan options because they are cheaper, in the long run, for the employer as well. In my past places of employment, I've received up to $2,000 per year from my employer for selecting a high deductible plan for my family. That's $2,000 of tax free money in an HSA that I can use for any health care related expense at any time in the future.

As of this writing in 2022, an individual selecting a high deductible plan can contribute $3,650 per year to their HSA (note this amount includes any employer contribution). A family can contribute $7,300 per year. Those 55 years old or older can contribute an additional $1,000 per year.

Don't miss the long term wealth building aspect of an HSA!

Here's the important part most people miss: to maximize the value of the aforementioned tax benefits, you really want to use your HSA account *like a retirement account* and not, as most people use it, as a fund to pay for ongoing, current medical costs. Most people set up their HSA and then use that account, with its handy HSA debit card all HSA's provide, to pay as they go throughout the course of the year to cover any medical costs that arise. While that is perfectly fine (it's frankly how these plans are designed to work), by doing this you lose the massive tax-free compounding power these plans can provide. Instead, to the extent you can afford to, try to pay your ongoing medical expenses out of your pocket, not your HSA account. Max out, again to the extent you can afford to, your annual contributions to your HSA and let that tax free money compound and grow.

When taking this course of action, you will need to maintain a file of all your ongoing out of pocket medical expenses while the HSA is accumulating. For simplicity, my wife keeps a folder of each year's medical receipts and then periodically loads them on a simple spreadsheet. The total on that spreadsheet provides backup for the future when we want to tap those HSA funds: as long as the accumulated out of pocket medical expenses match or exceed what you are withdrawing from the HSA account, you can spend that money on anything you want in the future. It's all tax free and you've got proper documentation to show that.

HSA accounts can be invested just like any other investment account. For example, I have my HSA account with HSA Bank which, in turn, allowed me to set up an investment account with TD Ameritrade. With that account, I can use my HSA funds to invest in stocks, ETFs, or mutual funds and that's exactly what I do. These then grow just like any of my other accounts, doubling accordingly over time.

One of the biggest concerns people have about pulling the plug and retiring early is how they will cover their health care costs before medicare kicks in at age 65. Wouldn't it be great to arrive at the time you want to retire at, say age 60, and have $50 or $100k sitting in an HSA account that can be used to fund most or all of your health care expenses during this bridge period? That's what I've done. You should consider it also. And the beauty is, Uncle Sam doesn't get his greedy fingers on a single penny of these hard earned dollars ever… as long as the funds are spent on medical expenses.

Step 6: Once you have the above covered, the next good investment option to think about is a Roth IRA.

The distinction between Roth IRAs and Roth 401ks and their non-

Roth versions is that you pay the taxes *upfront* on your contributions in both Roth IRAs and Roth 401ks, so you lose the tax deferral advantage you get with the traditional IRA and 401k noted earlier.

The huge advantage of a Roth is that, although your contributions are made after tax, the future appreciation on a Roth investment is never taxed as long as certain rules are followed. A traditional non-Roth IRA or 401k is taxed whenever you withdraw the funds in the future, at normal income tax rates (plus a 10% early withdrawal penalty if you withdraw funds before age 59 1/2).

For Roth (IRA/ or 401k) withdraws to be tax free, you need to be at least 59 1/2 before you withdraw funds, and the funds must have resided in a Roth account a minimum of 5 years. If you assume your tax rate is lower now than it will be when you retire (the younger you are, the better those odds are), the Roth IRA or Roth 401k alternative can be a good option to consider.

There are other advantages of a Roth IRA in terms of required minimum distributions (RMD-Roth IRAs have no required minimum withdrawal ever) as well as those related to estate planning, which are beyond the scope of this discussion. There is a lot of good information online that can explain these differences...simply Duck Duck Go "differences between Roth and traditional IRAs and 401ks" for a variety of sources on this topic. The bottom line is the tax implications of your investment choices are important to consider and understand.

Step 7: Put your savings and investments on "Auto Pilot."

As discussed, the smart way to invest, in order to ensure you are not buying and selling at the worst time, is to dollar cost average your investments AND THEN LET THEM RIDE. Whether it's your 401k or HSA contributions, which come directly out of your paycheck each pay period, or your personal investment contributions, which come out of your checking account on a monthly basis, these regular, timed investments set you up for automatic dollar cost averaging.

As I mentioned earlier, the other advantage to investing in this manner is that when you have the money coming out of your paycheck and checking account automatically, you mentally adjust to not having that money available to spend and, as a result, you tend to spend less...you adjust to the fewer dollars being available, and that is a huge help to building wealth.

Pop Quiz:
Here is a pop quiz, based on the above discussion of risk and reward associated with equities, bonds, and cash....

1. If your major financial goal is to save enough money for a downpayment to buy a new house within the next 2 two years, where should these savings be invested?
   ____Equities ____Bonds _____Cash

2. If you just had a child and want to start saving for college 18 years hence, where should the bulk of these savings be invested?
   ____Equities ____Bonds ____Cash

3. If you are 30 and your company offers a 401k with a variety of investment options and you plan to retire at age 60, where should the bulk of your 401k savings be invested?
   ____Equities ____Bonds ____Cash

Answers: The above questions each deal with the time horizon of your major goals at that stage of your life. Generally, the nearer term the goal (I use less than three years) the more you want to protect against short term volatility. For question 1, the answer is Cash. For question 2, the answer is Equities. For question 3, the answer is Equities.

Question 1: the safest bet to ensure you have the money to meet your goal is to put it in a savings or money market account where your principle is not at risk. There's no doubt stocks have the potential to get you to your goal faster, but they can also set achieving your goals back by several years if the market declines.

As an example of this, I will use the stock of a company I worked for, Owens Illinois (ticker symbol "OI" on the New York Stock Exchange). I started working at OI in early 2000, right before the general stock market melted down in the "Dot Com Bust". When I joined OI the stock was roughly $20 per share. By the end of 2000, due to the market meltdown as well as some other company-specific issues, the stock was trading at under $3 per share. By 2007, when I exited OI, the stock had rebounded to around $33 per share.

OI's stock is a great example of the volatility in stocks. Let's say that when I joined OI, if I was saving for a down payment on a house and if I had put all my downpayment money into OI stock at the beginning of 2000, by early 2001 I would have lost 85% of my money when the stock declined from $20 to $3 per share! The key point here is **when** you need your money drives much of the decision on **how** you should invest it.

Question 2: here, there is a much longer time horizon…the longer the timeframe you have to save until you need the money (in this case, 18 years until you start paying tuition), the more you want to weight your investment to what will generate the highest long term average return, which is equities. As your child gets older and closer to starting college, you want to adjust your college savings investments to more conservative investments, so more bonds and less equities. Finally, as your child gets within 2-3 years of starting college, you want to switch to more of a cash position so the money is guaranteed to be there when you need to start writing those tuition checks.

Question 3: like question 2 with an even longer time horizon-30 years until you plan to retire. Here, you definitely want to leverage the long term returns of equities to your advantage. You will surely endure some significant ups and downs in your portfolio over this time frame, but the long term historic averages show that equities will yield the biggest pile of money by the time you reach your golden years.

Step 8: So how do I actually invest the above savings?

Here's where the rubber meets the road. I am going to suggest a basic way to invest your money. Note-once again, I am not a financial planner or advisor, so do your own homework and make sure you are comfortable with any investments you make. Remember, the higher the return, the more volatility. And always keep in mind that past history is no guarantee of future performance on any investment.

If you follow the above priorities, you can see that as your savings grow, you will end up having several types of accounts over time:

- An emergency fund in a savings or money market account.
- Funds earmarked for upcoming major purchases (house, car, remodeling, etc.) also in a savings or money market account.
- 401k or 403b accounts for you and your spouse, if married, that are invested in mutual funds which are largely invested in equities and ideally equity index funds, especially if you have a long time horizon until retirement.
- An HSA account with a cash portion to cover your planned near term medical costs. If you can pay medical costs out of pocket, it's ideal to have your HSA money also invested in stocks or stock index mutual funds to take advantage of the awesome tax advantages noted.
- A Roth IRA largely invested in stock index mutual funds or ETFs.
- And finally, regular (not tax advantaged) investments. Again,

my advice is to have these in low cost index mutual funds or ETFs.

The above list of accounts might seem pretty complicated or overwhelming but it's really not:

- Your emergency funds and those funds that are earmarked for major planned expenses, once funded, just kind of sit there.
- The funds that go into the 401k/403b and HSA are on autopilot: they come out of each paycheck.
- You make your Roth determination each year based on your available money to invest and your expected income that year. Over a certain income ($144,000 if single and $214,000 if married filing jointly in 2022), you are not allowed to make Roth contributions.
- After you've made your Roth contribution determination for a given year, you can determine if you have excess savings that you want to contribute to a regular (not tax advantaged) investment account. For both the Roth and regular accounts, you can set up regular deductions from your checking account to fund these accounts. You also put these on autopilot.

How should I allocate between stocks and bonds?

Once these various accounts are set up, it's important to look at the total picture of all of your accounts and make sure your total portfolio allocation (ie how much is in stocks, bonds, etc.) is in line with the overall allocation you want it to be.

Keeping in mind, I have a fairly high risk tolerance and have always been a more aggressive investor, here are my suggestions to consider. These allocations always must take into account you having your emergency fund and funds for major purchases secure in a non-risky savings or money market account! When you are first starting out, your entire savings may be in your emergency fund and in that situation you would have zero money invested in stocks.

Age	Stock	Combined Bond/ Cash Allocation
Under 30	90-95%	5-10%
30-40	75-90%	10-25%
40-50	65-80%	20-35%
50-60*	55-75%	25-45%
Over 60/Retirement*	40-65%	35-60%

- As you get closer to retirement, the percent is impacted by how much you have accumulated compared to your living expenses. For example, If you have a nest egg of $5 million and your annual living expenses are "only" $100k, you can afford to be more aggressive with your stock allocation because you can most likely afford to weather a major market downturn. Your allocation also depends on if you have other sources of income such as social security and/or a pension. Having other sources of income can allow you to be more aggressive in your equity allocation.

Step 9: Invest your money-investment examples!

Once you've determined how you want to allocate your total portfolio among the different asset class allocations, you need to determine what investments you are going to allocate your money towards.

Here are some examples to consider; from an extremely simple (but still effective) autopilot approach to a more customized approach. Both of these examples are based on the points I've covered above. You can get way more complicated but, as discussed, it will not necessarily result in better returns over the long run.

Option 1: Simple "Auto-Pilot" approach

Many 401k, IRA, and individual investment accounts offer target date mutual fund options. With these types of funds, you can simply have all your money invested into a single "target date" fund, which includes investments that are indexed to match both stock and bond market performance. These target date funds typically hold a globally diversified stock index fund as well as a globally diversified bond index fund.

The allocation made by the fund between stocks and bonds changes and gets more conservative over time as you age. You pick the target date fund based on your age and rough anticipated retirement year. Many fund families, including Vanguard and Fidelity, offer these types of investments and they are auto-pilot investing personified.

For example, say you are 30 years old in 2022 and your 401k offers Vanguard as a fund provider. A simple option would be to invest all your dollars into the Vanguard Target Retirement 2055 Fund since you have about 35 years to age 65. This fund is actually composed of 5 other Vanguard funds (you can check the details at vanguard.com) of which ~90% are currently (at the person in this example's present age of 30) allocated to equities (60% US stocks/40% international stock index funds) with the remaining 10% allocated towards bonds (65% US bonds and 35% international bond index funds).

By investing in this way, your investments are highly diversified both in terms of the number of individual stocks these funds own as well as geographically. In the past year, as of 6/30/21, this particular fund increased by 36.4% (not too shabby). On average, over the past 10 years, it has increased 10.72% per year (doubling roughly every 6.7 years...again, not too shabby). Annual expenses for this fund are 0.15%/year, which are pretty low.

For simplicity, you can't beat these target date funds. To the extent your company offers a target date fund option, you could potentially put 100% of your 401k and HSA contributions into this type of fund as well as any Roth IRA or regular investments you make on your own. By setting up all your various investments in this way, you would not have to worry so much about rebalancing your portfolio, as described below, because these target date funds automatically do that rebalancing for you: as you age, the fund adjusts the portfolio to hold more bonds and less stocks.

Option 2: Custom "Auto Pilot" approach

If you want a more refined investment allocation, where you can precisely adjust how much you have in stocks and bonds as well as what percent of your stocks and bonds are invested in the US versus internationally, you can use the types of index funds the target date funds utilize as a guide. You would then select the same or similar index funds offered by your 401k and HSA plans, and make these allocations yourself. In some cases, your 401k and HSA investment options will be more limited. If that's the case, defaulting to a target date fund may be the best and easiest option for these dollars you have to invest.

For your Roth IRA and regular individual investments, Vanguard, Fidelity, and many other companies offer a myriad of index fund and ETF options to consider where you can accomplish the same thing.

If you choose this more customized approach, the two things you need to decide are:

1. The total portfolio allocation between stocks and bonds/cash.
2. The allocation between US and international for your stock and bond funds.

Example of mutual funds I have used for many years:

Here's an example of some funds I use through Vanguard. This group of funds can serve as a great way for just about any investor to accomplish their wealth building goals and is perfect for this more customized approach:

Equity/Stock funds:

- Vanguard's Total Stock Market Index Admiral fund (symbol VTSAX). As of this writing, this fund holds shares in 3,935 US companies...essentially every publicly traded stock in the US in proportion to their value, so it closely mimics the performance of the total US stock market (not just the S&P 500 stocks).

- Vanguard's International Growth Investor fund (symbol VWIGX) focuses on a more finite group (as of this writing, shares in 123 non-US companies). Note, this is an actively managed fund and not an index fund and, as a result, the expense ratio (0.44%) is a bit higher. For a lower cost, international stock index fund (as opposed to being actively managed) option, you might consider Vanguard's FTSE All World Ex-US fund (symbol VFWAX) which has a .11% expense ratio and has generated 28.73% 1 year/7.88% 10 year returns.

Bond funds:

- Vanguard's Total Bond Market Index Admiral fund (symbol VBTLX) gives you a broad portfolio (as of this writing, the fund holds 10,099 different bonds) of investment grade US government and mortgage backed securities of various durations, so it mimics the broad performance of the US bond market.

- Vanguard's Total International Bond Index Admiral fund (symbol VTABX) provides broad diversified exposure to the investment grade international (ex US) bond market and includes government, corporate, and agency bonds. As of this writing, this fund holds 6,361 different bonds.

Why are these funds useful?

As discussed, diversification spreads your risk. These funds give you exposure to literally thousands of different stocks and bonds. These four funds also provide US vs international diversification on both bonds and stocks. If the US market is not doing so well, sometimes international markets will be doing better and vice versa. This spreads your risk as well as your opportunities for return.

These funds also provide a balance between stocks and bonds which, often times, move in the opposite direction. This also helps hedge your returns in the event of a major stock market downturn.

With these four funds, you can adjust the percentage you allocate between stocks and bonds as well as how much you want to allocate between the US and international markets. As you get older, you can simply adjust the allocations over time to match your desired level of exposure to stocks. I am not pushing Vanguard specifically, though it's an excellent company to work with and is known for both performance and very low costs. There are many other fund companies out there whom you can invest with, but keep an eye on their costs!

Portfolio Example: A hypothetical allocation for a 30 year old might be that he or she desires an 85%/15% allocation between stocks and bonds and a 75%/25% allocation between US and international investments. For reference only (**remember, there is never a guarantee of future performance)**, I've also shown the most recent 1 and 10 year average performance for these particular mutual funds:

Vanguard Fund.	Allocation	1 Year Ret.*.	10 Year Ret.*	Exp %
Total Stock Mkt (US)	64%	38.95%	15.15%	0.04%
International Growth	21%	36.75%	12.42%	0.44%
Total Bond Mkt (US)	11%	-0.76%.	3.22%.	0.05%
Total Int'l Bond	4%	0.51%	3.83%**	0.11%

Total Allocation For This Example: 100% with 85% in stocks and 15% in bonds

*Fund performance is through 6/30/21 per Vanguard.

** Since fund inception on 5/31/13

Step 10: Fund rebalancing & portfolio adjustments as you age (Note-You don't have to do this and can skip this part if you use the Option 1 Auto-pilot approach with target date funds)

As you can see from the above performance results, each fund listed will grow at a different rate. In a bull market, the stock funds will grow way faster than your bond funds. During a bear market, when stocks can decline significantly, your bond funds will typically hold up much better and, in some cases, grow while your stock funds fall in value. Because of these changing and dynamic results, it's important you check your investment allocations and rebalance these from time to time. To keep it simple, I'd look at this at least on an annual basis.

For example, if you find that, after a bull market year, your stocks are now 90% of your total portfolio instead of your desired 85% allocation in the example above, you might consider taking 5% of your stock portfolio and allocating it across your bond funds so that your allocation is back at your desired mix.

Try to avoid a tax hit when you adjust your allocations!

If possible, make these rebalancing adjustments in your tax deferred accounts (IRA, 401k, etc.) or your HSA account, so you don't trigger any taxes owed.

You should also rebalance as needed to adjust for your allocation between US and international investments as these can sometimes also get out of whack. Again, **it's important you look across all your accounts to assess your total portfolio allocation when considering these rebalancing changes**, even if you only use your 401k account, (for example) to do the actual rebalancing to avoid a taxable event.

Here's an example of how you might assess this at the end of the year and make an adjustment that does not trigger taxes:

A 38 year old started a given year with a desired 90% stock/10% bond allocation with a target 75% US/25% international allocation using the above funds:

At the end of 2021 this investor finds the following totals in their various accounts (all $ in thousands)

	US Stock	Int'l Stock	US Bond	Int'l Bond
Regular Account	$150	$20	$10	$5
401k Account	$150	$70	$40	$15
IRA Account	$250	$150	$40	$25
HSA Account	$50	$10	$10	$5
Total:	$600	$250	$100	$50

You can see this person ended the year with a total portfolio across their various accounts worth $1m...not too shabby! However, they now only have $850k or 85% of their total portfolio in stocks (vs. the 90% they targeted). Also, their US/Int'l stock allocation is now 71%/29% vs the 75%/25% US/Int'l they targeted. Their bond allocation is now 67%/33% US/Int'l.

To rebalance and avoid triggering any taxable events this year, this person should reallocate funds as needed to get back to their desired allocations over their entire portfolio using their 401k, IRA and/or HSA accounts and not their regular (non tax-advantaged) account. One way to do this would be as follows:

- Move $25k from their 401k Int'l stock account to their 401k US stock account

- Move $25k from their 401k US bond account to their 401k US stock account
- Move $25k from their IRA Int'l bond account to their IRA US stock account

The result of these 3 moves will give the investor the following new totals:

	US Stock	Int'l Stock	US Bond	Int'l Bond
Individual Account	$150	$20	$10	$5
401k Account	$200	$45	$15	$15
IRA Account	$275	$150	$40	$0
HSA Account	$50	$10	$10	$5
Total:	$675	$225	$75	$25

Which gets this person back to their desired 90%/10% stock/bond allocation with both stocks and bonds allocated 75% to US investments and 25% to international investments.

Adjusting your stock/bond allocation as you age:
Unless you use a fully auto-pilot target date fund where the asset class allocation changes automatically as you age, you need to consider and potentially adjust your asset class allocations periodically (for example, every 5-10 years), getting a bit more conservative as you get closer to retirement.

Note: absolute precision is not required! If, when you look at your year-end portfolio you are only a few percent off your desired allocations, you don't need to necessarily make adjustments…that's your call. However, over time, you will generally find that stocks, bonds, and US and international investments each move differently in fairly significant ways, and if you don't review and rebalance your portfolio periodically, you will find you can be pretty far off from where you started.

Do I really have to do this boring math stuff?

You can save this work if you use target date funds for your investments. But if you elect to do the more customized approach where you are picking your own funds, then yes you should do this rebalancing every year or so.

This rebalancing requires a little bit of math and maybe an hour or so of your time each year, but I am confident if you are taking the time to read this book, it will be pretty easy for you. Doing this bit of work gives you a much better shot towards building significant wealth because it will allow you to avoid paying an advisor potentially hundreds of thousands of dollars or more over the course of your life.

The other advantage is that over time you will gain a solid understanding of your investments. I strongly believe that understanding will give you confidence when you decide to take the plunge and stop working for someone else full time.

If you find, after doing this rebalancing for a period of time, that you really don't like doing it, you can always elect to change your investments over to target date funds. Just try to avoid unnecessary taxes on your regular accounts when making such a conversion!

> **Life Hack #35: The above two approaches to investing (Option 1 simple autopilot using target date funds and Option 2 custom autopilot) take minimal time to understand and implement in your own life, but are really all you need to take ownership of managing your investments in an efficient, low cost way.**
>
> **History shows, over time, using index funds will most likely**

result in your financial returns being as good as or better than most professionally managed funds and at a fraction of the cost. It's that simple.

Can you go out and really study the markets, research individual companies, and pick your own stocks and bonds? Yes, you can, but the evidence shows you will likely do better by simply buying and holding index funds that match market performance, especially if you dollar cost average your money into these investments and let it ride over the long term.

Life Hack #36: Hubris Alert!!! The biggest reason individual investors as well as most professional stock pickers do not generally achieve investment returns similar or better than the market indexes is that they think they know more than the cumulative knowledge of all investors, as reflected in the current market price. This is called hubris.

The best way to ensure you *don't* match market performance is to try timing the market by pulling your money out when you think the economy and/or market is going to tank or invest a ton of money into the market when you think the market has bottomed and is going to take off.

Follow the steps above and dollar cost average your money into the market then let it ride...other than for periodic asset allocation rebalancing!

Chapter 14

Investment Advisors: Is Yours Earning Their Pay?

I have a passion to try and educate people on the basics of personal finance and their ability to manage their own investments. When you look at the costs of having an advisor manage your money over the course of your life and the performance an advisor historically has produced vs index funds, it's just not logical to me why someone would not want to have control over this important aspect of their future.

If you are using an advisor, are they earning their keep?

As I finish this book in early 2022, the financial results for 2021 have just gone in the books. With that being the case, here's a somewhat simple way for you to see if your advisor is earning their keep:

Measuring performance:

The best way to see if your advisor is earning what you're paying them is to compare their results against an objective market benchmark where you could have simply invested your money and let it ride (as I advocate). **For the three years ended on 12/31/21, the S&P 500 index slightly more than doubled**. That's right. If you had simply put your money in a low cost (~0.04% expense ratio) S&P 500 index mutual fund or ETF, it would be worth roughly double after three years without you lifting a finger.

Because of the simple math of the S&P 500 doubling over the last three years, it's easy for you to compare how your money grew if you were investing some other way: either picking stocks on your own or using an advisor.

Here's how you can estimate your performance vs. the market:

1. Write down what your account balance was on 12/31/18. Find your statement or check online.

2. Compare that to what your 12/31/21 balance is and write it down. Try to net out any deposits and withdrawals you made in this account during this timeframe so you are comparing the investment return during the three years only. Make sure that all fees and charges associated with your account are deducted from your final total so you are reflecting your net return after all expenses during this timeframe.

3. The difference between your 2018 and 2021 ending balances will show what your net return (profit) was over the past three years.

4. Compare the results to the S&P 500's results, which doubled during this timeframe.

5. Bottom Line-How are you or your advisor performing? If you started out on 12/31/18 with $100,000, that same amount of money in a S&P 500 index fund or ETF would now be worth roughly $200,000. Did the money you or your advisor invested double during this time? If not, it's worth figuring out why, isn't it?

Life Hack #37: Investing your hard earned savings is the serious business of building wealth for you and your family. You should always be striving to earn an investment return that is at least equal to the market. If you or your advisor are not consistently doing that, be a learning creature and consider a different approach.

Reasons you or your advisor are underperforming the market:

6. As noted earlier in the book, the market beats the vast majority (more than 94% over the past 20 years) of all professional stock pickers. If you or your advisor are picking stocks rather than

investing in market-based index funds, you will almost certainly lose over time. Period.

7. Costs: Your advisor will charge you many times more in fees and commissions than the cost of an index mutual fund or ETF. These costs come right out of your pocket and really add up over time. Even if your advisor is investing your money in a low cost index fund, the fact you are paying them 1-2% ***on top*** of the fund costs really adds up over time.

8. The other huge risk and potential cost of either you picking stocks, or having an advisor invest your money, is the risk you or they will try to time the market. The only way your money would have doubled in the S&P 500 over the last three years is if you would have put it in at the end of 2018 ***and left it there*** the entire three years. People, especially advisors, are always tempted to think they know better than everyone else and often move money in and out of the market, which essentially insures underperformance. **Let the money ride!**

My final word on advisors (promise!)

I've got nothing against people trying to make a living and some of my friends are investment advisors. For people who are absolutely not interested in understanding the simple basics of money or don't have the mental capability to manage their own money, advisors can provide a valuable service.

That being said, we all work hard for our money, and it's difficult for me to understand why people wouldn't want to invest a bit of time to learn the basics so they can ensure they will get to the financial promise land years sooner rather than potentially many years later.

The sooner your money can earn more than you do working each year, the sooner you will be able to emancipate yourself any time you choose. I'd never turn that extremely important responsibility over to someone else.

Bonus Chapter 15

Crypto and the Blockchain Revolution

You might ask yourself why I would include a chapter specifically on crypto…it might seem a bit out of place in this more general outline about the nuts and bolts of investing and building wealth. The reason is I believe crypto and, more specifically, blockchain technology is a real inflection point for not only the economy but also potentially the world. What's more, while I am far from an expert on crypto, survey's show the vast majority of the population, including those in developed countries like the US, know almost nothing about this game-changing technology.

I view crypto and its underlying blockchain technology similar to how one might have viewed electricity in the 1870s or the internet in the early 1990s: if you understood the potential of these world-changing technologies at that time when most people didn't, and you were writing a book about how to succeed and build wealth in the coming years, it would be kind of crazy to ignore the topic, right?

As such, given the earth-shaking potential I foresee, I'd be remiss if I didn't at least try to provide a brief outline of what I understand about crypto. This will be a brief sort of "blockchain for blockheads" overview, if you will. My hope is that this sparks some curiosity in you to learn more. For those interested, I've listed a few really good YouTube channels that cover crypto extensively in the reference section at the end of the book.

Isn't "crypto" the same as Bitcoin?

If you are asking this question, you need to read this chapter! This is akin to asking "isn't Amazon the same as the internet?" Bitcoin

(Which I'll refer to by its trading symbol BTC) is a pioneering cryptocurrency that has grown exponentially in value since its inception in 2008.

BTC is an asset that exists on a specific blockchain, and really the underlying blockchain technology established with BTC is the prototype for the entire crypto universe. A blockchain is a decentralized network that, at its core, is a ledger that allows for validation of transactions in a secure, anonymous way. While BTC has dramatically increased in value, it's the underlying blockchain technology that, to me, is world-changing.

Here's why in a nutshell: Throughout history, the way man has transacted things of value…from cavemen trading a pretty rock for a spear or hunk of meat, to you buying a new hat with your credit card, all these transactions involve you either making the deal directly with the other party or through a middleman who keeps track of the transactions, usually for a nice little fee:

- Your bank gets paid by the store that sells you the hat in return for processing the credit card transaction. Then they charge you, the buyer of the hat, interest if you don't pay them back in a timely manner.

- When you buy a house, you pay the realtor a commission as well as other parties like title companies and lawyers to facilitate the transaction in a risk free way.

- If you are from Nigeria and working in the US, you pay Western Union a percentage to send some of your pay back to your family in Africa.

- In addition to the middleman transaction costs, there is also a big element of trust involved in our historic transactions: do you trust the person you are doing a transaction with to follow through and actually pay you? Do you trust the financial institution won't get hacked? So, while most transactions do go through correctly, you have to rely on the other party to be both competent and honest in holding up their end of the bargain.

Blockchain technology changes all that: it gets rid of the middleman in the transactions and it gets rid of the need to trust the other party.

Think about that:

- What if you could sell or buy a house and not have any ancillary transaction costs involved in the purchase?
- What if you were a lender and you could loan your money to someone anywhere in the world risk free without any middlemen?
- What if you were part of the 2 billion people in the world who have no access to banks and can now do transactions safely and securely with anyone else in the world…how would that unlock the true human potential of all these people?

The fundamental aspect of the blockchain is it completely removes the need for person-to-person or institution-to-institution trust that heretofore was always required in all transactions. It's a completely "trust-less" system, and that is one of the key attributes that makes it revolutionary. Hopefully, your mind is getting a little bit blown now and you're asking, how does the blockchain do all this?

Revolutionary accounting?

At its core, a blockchain does accounting which, to most folks, is pretty boring. In a traditional system such as you lending money to a friend or a bank lending you money for a car purchase, each of the participants involved in the transaction keeps track of who owes what to whom. If one of the parties dies, skips town, or simply decides not to honor the deal, the other party is at risk. Lawyers and courts end up sorting out the mess.

A blockchain is really, at its essence, a way to track transactions in a fool-proof way, where trusting or even knowing the other party is not required. In the BTC blockchain, as described below, (not all blockchains work in exactly the same way) it does this by having many independent people running, in some cases, many thousands of computers that verify each transaction. Each transaction only gets approved if every single one of those computers come to a consensus that the transaction is valid.

Why would anyone invest in a bunch of high speed computers to do this mundane accounting? Because they earn some of the cryptocurrency they are validating as compensation for providing this fundamental service to the network...earning currency in return for processing and validating transactions on the blockchain is what's called "mining."

It's easy to go down a rabbit hole into any single element of crypto blockchains; the intent here is to provide the basics. The heart of crypto is the blockchain which regulates and validates transactions, and since the introduction of BTC, with its own unique blockchain, other cryptocurrencies have come onto the market with their own blockchains. A key differentiator to be aware of is the ways each of these cryptocurrency blockchains validate transactions. Many have modified ways of validating transactions...and some are more secure than others.

All of these cryptocurrencies are working at balancing tradeoffs in their blockchains, which have come to be known as the sinister sounding crypto trilemma.

The crypto trilemma

Since the introduction of BTC, thousands of other cryptos have entered the market, most with their own blockchains, rules and, in many cases, methods of validating transactions. As this has all unfolded, a "trillemma" has become apparent in terms of the fundamental tradeoffs each blockchain makes, and these are important to note if you decide to dip your toe in the water and invest in cryptos. The trilemma represents three somewhat opposing tradeoffs each blockchain has to make:

Security: There are now a variety of ways different blockchains validate transactions. The BTC and Ethereum (symbol ETH) blockchains utilize what is called the Proof of Work method of validating transactions. ETH is the second largest crypto in terms of market capitalization. Another way to validate transactions is called Proof of History, which is used by some newer coins such as Solana (symbol SOL). The Proof of History method does not require consensus from all the miners, instead it focuses on each miner agreeing on the history of a transaction. The tradeoff with Solana's approach is it can be less secure and, in fact, the Solana network has had two major hacks just in 2021 alone.

Speed: The reason Solana and many other cryptos would choose a less secure validation protocol is speed, and speed translates to lower transaction costs. BTC and ETH's highly secure Proof of Work method is slow and transactions are somewhat costly. Solana's blockchain, on the other hand, has the potential to process transactions at the same speed as Visa, which opens up the real opportunity to compete against traditional financial networks in terms of volume and cost per transaction.

While ETH, like BTC, has, up to this point, used the bullet-proof Proof of Work method to validate transactions, ETH is moving to a "Proof of Stake" validation method in the next year or so. This change in validation method is critical for the ETH network. It will improve the number of transactions ETH can handle and reduce transaction costs, which currently are extremely high. We get into the weeds a bit here but, basically, in Proof of Work, miners compete by working to solve complex problems using their computers. Those who are the best and fastest at this are rewarded with crypto as they validate transactions on the blockchain. This competition takes time and consumes massive amounts of computing power across many miners' computer systems and, as a result, consumes lots of energy.

Proof of Stake, instead, eliminates miners per se and replaces them with people who serve as validators. These people stake/invest their own Ethereum coin as collateral in order to set up a system where they will manage one of Ethereum's Proof of Stake nodes. Each of these decentralized nodes securely handles transactions on the blockchain. The staked collateral each node validator has invested in the network serves as a disincentive for dishonest or otherwise poor management of their node: the validator runs the risk of losing some or all of their staked coin based on rules built into the blockchain.

This conversion of Ethereum from Proof of Work to Proof of Stake is known as "ETH 2.0" and is a hugely anticipated event. Currently, a person must stake (invest as collateral) 32 ETH, currently worth about $110,000, in order for them to become a validator of an ETH 2.0 node. Each validator, as such, has skin in the game to ensure they operate the node as required by the blockchain. If they don't operate within the rules of the blockchain the validator risks losing the crypto they have staked. In turn, the validator earns a return on the ETH they have staked (presently in the 5-8% range while ETH 2.0 is currently being finalized...ETH 2.0 is due to launch sometime in 2022 or 2023).

Once ETH 2.0 goes live, the validators will earn fees based on each transaction they validate. Because Proof of Stake eliminates the computing competition amongst miners, it reduces computing power and energy consumption. A question remains as to whether or not this method will be as secure as Proof of Work...many believe it will not be. Proof of Stake will, however, allow for much faster and less expensive transactions, and this is the driver behind Ethereum moving to this consensus method in the future.

Decentralization: This is a biggie. A huge part of the original impetus for BTC and the whole crypto movement has been to disconnect from centralized control in any form: whether that be a central government, a large corporation, or a greedy billionaire.

BTC is a truly decentralized system: no one owns it and no individual controls it. The BTC blockchain is "socially enforced" meaning the only way the underlying rules, including how many BTC can ever be mined, is that 100% of the nodes (more than 10,000 currently) all agree to the change.

A node on the BTC blockchain maintains a computer where the entire history of the blockchain resides. Each node has veto power over any proposed changes to the underlying rules of the blockchain as well as provides oversight on the miners validating specific blockchain transactions. Having 10,000 independent nodes ensures one or a small group of actors cannot highjack the blockchain for their own ends.

With the recent gold rush of capital flowing into blockchains and cryptos, many coins are not nearly as decentralized as BTC. Solana, as one example, has hundreds of millions invested in it by a small group of venture capital investors and, as a result, this raises genuine concerns about its level of decentralization and integrity in the long term: are these investors' interests completely aligned with Solana coin holders?

Bottom line, most blockchains need to focus on at most two of the three legs of the crypto trilemma as it's difficult, if not impossible, to achieve all three. Many newer coins are trading some level of security for faster speeds, better energy utilization, and lower transaction costs.

Bitcoin..the granddaddy and gold standard of cryptos

Now is a good time to go back and explain a bit more about BTC specifically, what makes it tick and why it has become so valuable. The truly brilliant and revolutionary introduction of BTC by someone calling themselves Satoshi Nakamoto in 2008, not only established the coin itself but also, as noted, the concept of the blockchain that has now spawned thousands of other coins and blockchain platforms.

As mentioned above, these coins and blockchains are not all the same. **Read that again: these coins and blockchains are not all the same.** BTC and its underlying blockchain are unique in several ways from other cryptocurrencies:

- First, BTC was designed as a truly decentralized platform... no company owns it, and the only way the guiding rules of how BTC operates can be changed is if all the node operators agree to those changes.
- BTC, by design from its inception, will only ever have a total of 21 million coins.
- The BTC protocol also periodically "halves" the payments miners earn for validating transactions. In other words, when one of these "halving" events occur, which happens every four years, a miner needs to perform twice the number of transactions to earn the same amount of bitcoin compared to before the halving.
- This in turn, slows the rate new BTC is produced and enters the marketplace. The last halving occurred on May 11, 2020.
- Currently, about 18 million BTC have been mined. The continued reduction in BTC production, because of these periodic halving events, means that the last 3 million of the total 21 million BTC will not be mined until around 2140..that's right: 120 years from now!
- One of the things that makes BTC unique in the crypto world is this limited supply: there will never be more than 21 million BTC unless all the nodes agree there should be more. Given that would dilute and decrease the value of BTC, that is extremely unlikely.
- The other key thing that makes BTC unique is the way its blockchain operates and how transactions are validated. As

noted, BTC uses a consensus protocol called Proof of Work. The good thing about this method is that it is absolutely secure and almost unhackable. The bad thing is validating using Proof of Work is slow and highly energy intensive in computer terms and, as a result, limits the numbers of transactions that can be handled in a given amount of time. Speed also translates to cost per transaction. It's not uncommon for a single BTC transaction to take several minutes to complete. By comparison, the Visa credit card network handles up to 400,000 transactions **per second.**

- From this brief overview, you can hopefully get a sense of the value and limitations of BTC:

Bitcoin pros:

It has limited supply: Unlike the supply of US dollars which has increased over 37% during the past two years, BTC will never have more than 21 million coins. Also, it's estimated that roughly 20%, or 3-4 million, BTC has been lost since its inception meaning that in all likelihood, only 17-18 million coins will ever exist.

It's secure: As described, the Proof of Work validation method is as bullet proof as any method in existence.

It's decentralized: Not one person, company, or government owns or controls BTC. Governments, big banks, and lots of other powerful entities hate this aspect of BTC, and cryptocurrency in general.

It's anonymous: While there is a history of each coin's life and all the transactions its gone through, no one can know who owns which specific coins, and you never know who you are transacting with unless you do that outside the network on a peer to peer basis.

It's portable: You can have your cryptocurrency, like BTC, on a network such as Coinbase (which in essence is like a crypto bank account), or you can have it accessible through a cold wallet. A cold wallet is simply a device that looks like a USB thumb drive, which retains your security keys to access the coins you own on the blockchain offline. The coins themselves always remain on the blockchain but an owner's specific coins can only be accessed by using secure keys (typically a series of words). When you connect your cold wallet to the internet to access your coins, it becomes a "hot" wallet.

The reason people have "lost" their BTC in the past is because they have lost their security keys. Because the blockchain is totally decentralized, there is no one else who's able to replace or reset your keys if you lose them. While the coins still exist on the blockchain, they are forever unretrievable by you or anyone else without those keys.

Due to its scarcity and security, many people equate BTC to gold as an asset that serves as a store of value. A huge advantage of BTC is you can travel anywhere in the world with your cold wallet and it could provide access to literally millions or billons of dollars worth of BTC. With gold, you'd need a truck to move that much value.

The portability aspect of BTC has really shown its value in the current Ukraine conflict: with many Ukrainians losing their homes and access to bank accounts, and fleeing the war, some were able to easily transport their wealth if it was held in Bitcoin. There have been countless stories of how BTC has provided a real lifeline to these people, which no bank or government can take away because the BTC blockchain is not controlled by any government or institution.

Another example of the value of holding assets on the BTC blockchain is the recent horrendous totalitarian freezing and seizure of peoples' bank accounts by the Canadian government in retaliation for citizens simply donating to a cause that protested the government's draconian Covid policies. If these same folks had retained some of their assets on the BTC blockchain, government seizure of these assets would not have been possible.

Bitcoin cons:

Due to the rigorous Proof of Work validation and consensus method, the BTC network is very slow and energy intensive, and transactions are not cheap. This is the big drawback of using BTC for everyday transactions.

Here's another thing that bothers some people who have studied BTC: they contend the whole Satoshi Nakamoto origin story could really be propaganda and Bitcoin could have actually been created by the CIA, WEF, or some other nefarious government entity, to help facilitate the "you will own nothing and be happy" globalist objective. This theory contends the government will be able to track all transactions as they will all be on the blockchain. As part of this concern, they note how "coincidental" it was that Bitcoin came into being right as the financial world was melting down in the 2008 financial crisis, and the "individual" who created it "vanished" right after creating it! Bitcoin plays into the whole notion of an orchestrated "Great Reset".

This is a concern that also extends to emerging government-sponsored stable coins where potentially governments would directly control all of their citizens' money. These coins would be electronically tracked. So the concern is that money could be frozen and confiscated instantly, without proper due process if, for example, a given citizen doesn't say or do exactly what the government wants them to (which I will coin the phrase here as "doing a Trudeau!").

Bottom line: Fears of insidious global control aside, BTC has evolved to being used primarily as a store of value investment for the reasons mentioned above. Due to its highly secure but slow and somewhat costly way of validating transactions, its become less valuable or practical as a way of actually transacting every day purchases.

Note, there are "level two" platforms that have been developed and are being implemented to further enhance and mitigate the transaction speed issue with the BTC blockchain. A level two platform sits on top of the original blockchain architecture (which is called a level one platform)...whether that be for BTC or another coin.

For the BTC blockchain, the leading level two platform is called the lightening network. The lightening network seeks to make transaction speeds approach those in the Visa credit card network and this, in turn, would allow BTC to be more practical to use for a much broader range of transactions.

Smart Contracts: As I explained earlier, BTC, due to its high level of security, finite supply of coins, and slow transaction speeds has largely evolved, at least for the time being, as a store of value. A host of other coins, led by Ethereum, have pioneered a whole new level of blockchain functionality called smart contracts.

Essentially, these coins contain embedded code that allows them to execute a set of specific instructions as part of each transaction. If each of the conditions defined by these instructions is not present, the transaction is not executed.

Again, I don't want to get too far into the weeds in how all this works but, as an example, let's say you are a farmer in Africa who has heretofore never had access to a bank, let alone a crop insurance company, to insure your current season's planting against drought:

- With a smart contract on Ethereum as well as some other blockchains, the farmer could stake some agreed upon number of coins as the premium for the desired insurance (as defined above, staking means providing coins as collateral for the transaction). These staked coins are held on the blockchain until the conditions of the smart contract transaction are finally determined.

- The "insurance provider" (which, on the blockchain, could really be anyone who wants to take a risk on providing this insurance), in this example, would also stake the amount of coin required to fully pay the farmer in the event of a drought (the terms of which would be known by both parties and embedded in the code for that smart contract).

- An independent information source defined in the terms of the smart contract would provide the blockchain with relevant rainfall and other pertinent weather data to determine if drought conditions in fact occurred.

- At the end of the season, the conditions embedded in the smart contract (not a human or potentially greedy company) would assess the agreed upon data.

- If the conditions indicated the farmer was adversely impacted by the weather as outlined in the terms of the smart contract, the blockchain would release the coins staked by the insurance provider to the farmer.

- If, on the other hand, the weather parameters indicated a normal harvest due to weather should have been possible, the coins staked by the farmer as the premium would go to the insurer.

Trust-less Contracts

There is no human involved to change their mind and decide not to pay the farmer. There is no opportunity for an unethical person or company to simply take the farmer's money and skip town. From the entity providing the insurance's perspective, there is no chance they won't get paid their premium due to the farmer going bankrupt or deciding not to pay.

Once the smart contract is initiated by both parties on the blockchain, both the premium and policy amounts are fully locked into the blockchain. Hence, this is a fully trust-less and risk-free system for all the participants: you don't need to know, meet with, or have trust in the person you are transacting the business with. You are relying on the blockchain to hold the funds until the parameters of the smart contract are fulfilled.

Here's the other huge aspect of blockchains in general, and smart contracts in particular: the "insurance company" in the above example doesn't have to be an actual "insurance company." It could be anyone who has an interest in the African farmer or wants to take a risk on insuring his farm against drought in order for a fair return.

Blockchains get rid of the stranglehold monopolies we currently have over all kinds of businesses...from insurance companies to banks to art auction houses to real estate companies to record labels. Regular people from across the world will be able to borrow, buy, lend, or invest in all manner of things using developing blockchain platforms. This is revolutionary and has the potential to unlock the power and creativity of a much larger swath of the world's population in a much more efficient way by eliminating the greedy middlemen currently involved in all of these types of transactions today.

NFTs

Here is another example. You may have heard about non fungible tokens known as NFTs. While the current hype in the media relates to some crazy rich person paying millions for an NFT cartoon of a monkey or some such thing, NFTs are examples of smart contracts and will change many facets of the economy in the coming years.

An NFT could represent title of ownership to just about anything; it could be art, a song, or, crazy as it may sound, your house in the future. For example, let's say you are selling your beautiful lake house because you need to move elsewhere for work. You regret having to sell it because you know it's a great property that will keep appreciating. In the not too distant future, when you can sell property on a blockchain with a smart contract using an NFT, you might mutually agree to give the buyer of your lake house a lower price now in return for every time the lake house is sold in the future, you get 10% of any appreciation on the house...forever.

In this example, the buyer gets the benefit of a better price now and the seller gets the future potential benefit that he will share in any appreciation of the house, forever. The "deed" for the house would reside as an NFT in a perpetual smart contract on the blockchain, and any time the conditions of the smart contract are met (in this case, the house gets sold in the future), the blockchain would calculate the appreciation of the house since the last sale and release an appropriate number of coins to the original seller which would reflect their agreed upon share of the appreciation. What will happen to the 5-7% commission the greedy real estate company middleman currently enjoys when they sell a house? It's going to be largely gone, putting more money in the buyer's and seller's pockets.

While the above real estate transaction example may sound pretty far-fetched, similar transactions with art NTFs are happening today. An artist who creates a work of art sells it to a buyer using an NFT with a smart contract that continues to pay the artist a specific percentage of any growth in value of the work of art forever into the future. Every time that piece of art sells down the road, the artist will automatically get their agreed upon percentage. Musical compositions are also starting to follow the same path (my son has already monetized some of the music he's produced utilizing NFTs that are transacted on the ETH blockchain).

Here's a recent real world example: in early February, 2022, Alfa Romeo introduced a new SUV. Each car comes with its own unique NFT that that will track vehicle data, which can be used to generate a certificate to prove the car has been properly maintained. Alfa Romeo believes this will enhance each car's resale value.

Are you excited about cryptos yet?

I'm really hoping your mind is a little bit blown now:

- For the 2 billion people in the world who have no access to a bank, let alone insurance, blockchain and smart contract options allow these people to be participants in the global economy with access to capital and a secure, inexpensive way to move capital and transact business.

- For artists and creators, it allows them the potential to capture a much fairer share of the fruits of their labors and to create new future revenue streams.
- For everyone, it provides a much broader opportunity to invest in all kinds of things heretofore reserved for the rich, and giant corporations...not just investing in a piece of digital art of monkeys, but it also gives them the ability to invest directly in the farmer in Africa who needs crop insurance.

Turning the current world order on its head

Guess who's not too happy about all this? You guessed it: all the guys who have been in control and raking in trillions of dollars for years. The banks, insurance companies, music companies, real estate companies, and other businesses that, throughout history, have been deciding who gets what while getting a big slice of the pie on just about every transaction that occurs for themselves.

Governments are also very concerned (see China's attempt in 2021 to make cryptos illegal...other than their own digital yuan of course!) because all of these transactions flow through highly decentralized networks that have thousands of nodes of redundancy built in, so they aren't easy to shut down or control.

Blockchains will provide much more efficient and cost effective ways of transacting lots of types of business. And smart contracts embedded in these blockchains will protect and de-risk the transaction for both the buyer and seller.

Hopefully, you now have a glimpse of what all the hubbub is about with cryptos, blockchains, and smart contracts. Like almost all aspects in the crypto universe, it's a dynamic environment with massive amounts of interest and capital flowing into the market. Where things will land in the future is unknown. Hence, all cryptos, including BTC, are highly volatile and risky, but the potential value these developments hold is massive, revolutionary, and will be transformational.

To those who understand all this, there are still early adopter opportunities. As of this writing, only 11% of Americans are invested in any way in crypto, and in most cases it's in BTC which, as you now understand, is a very limited part of the entire blockchain universe.

But make no mistake, the traditional world of finance and government powers are waking up to the massive efficiencies and freedom blockchain technology has the potential to provide:

- If you are a major bank, you'd rightly be terrified if blockchains can eliminate the need for you as a middleman to arrange a car or home loan. You'd be working hard to try and figure out how you can use this technology to maintain your little fiefdom of wealth and power.

- If you're a major insurance company, you'd be very worried if it became possible through a blockchain to secure insurance for someone's life, their crops, or their car, directly from individuals willing to take that risk in return for a reasonable return.

- If you're one of the three major music companies, you'd feel vulnerable if artists could directly connect and sell their music to fans, capturing a fairer share of the value of the work they produce compared to the peanuts the music industry currently pays artists. In addition, it opens the opportunity for music fans to invest in artists they like and share in the proceeds that artist earns in the future.

Unlocking everyone's full potential

It's an exciting time to be alive, and I firmly believe this will be transformative in almost miraculous ways by: unlocking human potential around the world, fueling a capitalist renaissance that has the potential to lift many out of poverty, and empowering millions to take a much more direct role in the global economy, giving fairer access to everyone to attain a higher level of prosperity.

Most people still view Bitcoin, blockchains, and crypto as all being the same thing. They can't wrap their brain around the fact a "coin" that doesn't actually physically exist can be worth anything, let alone $60,000 or more. Most have never stopped to think about the fact the paper dollar in their wallet also, actually, doesn't have any intrinsic value other than what other people assign that value to be.

The fact the US government has had a longstanding policy of expanding the money supply (a dollar in the early 1950s is now only worth about $.10!), which has gone into hyperdrive since the pandemic, makes those who've studied the situation more inclined to invest some of their capital in a crypto like Bitcoin, which has a fixed supply vs an ever depreciating dollar.

For new or casual investors: my advice is don't invest in cryptos

While I believe there is huge potential in cryptos generally, it's impossible to predict which cryptos will really succeed in the future. Because of this, cryptos are an extremely risky investment and should not be part of your basic investing game plan, which were discussed in the preceding "You Incorporated" chapters.

Experienced investors:

If you're an experienced investor with a diversified portfolio that currently goes beyond stocks and bonds and includes a small allocation in precious metals, you might consider the approach I take to investing in cryptos. I initially started investing in cryptos in late 2017, basically dabbling with a very small amount of money to begin with.

As I've learned more about blockchains and the crypto ecosystem that's evolving, I've expanded my crypto allocation to where I now own five different coins that each have somewhat different value propositions. These include Bitcoin, Ethereum, Chainlink, Solana, and Polkadot. See the suggested references at the back of the book to learn more about crypto and these specific coins. From an overall portfolio standpoint, I view the amount I'm allocating (currently about 3-4% of my total portfolio) into the crypto market similar to how I would look at an allocation in gold or other precious metals. Like gold, it's a good hedge against further devaluation of the dollar and, also like gold, crypto's performance does not really seem to be correlated with the stock and bond markets.

Because there's still a very low level of adoption and understanding of cryptos, and such high potential as outlined above, I view investing in these assets as a way to diversify a small part of my portfolio and provide the potential for outsized returns with the knowledge that there is also huge downside potential in both the short and long run.

Chapter 16

Emancipation!

Last year, I entered what I call the "emancipation" stage of my career. While this term is frequently associated with being freed from slavery, it also means being set free from dependence and liberation from a controlling influence so, to me, it fits with intentionally exiting working for someone else.

I choose not to use the term "retired" because, honestly, that does not fit where I am at on a lot of different levels. To me, "retired" means electing to be put out to pasture, to ripen and rot on a porch swing or while riding around on a golf cart. That's probably a little harsh and at some point I will probably want to completely quit working but at the present time, that's not me by a long shot.

"Emancipation" is a term that better fits my current situation: I've freed myself from permanently working for someone else and now have the freedom to choose how, when, and what I work on and how much time I want to devote to that activity. I'm not done "working," I'm just done doing it in the conventional sense, at the beck and call of someone else.

My wish is for you to be able to experience emancipation sometime in the future as well…hopefully as early in your life as you desire… and that your emancipation will fulfill all your wishes and dreams.

So how do you emancipate?

There are building blocks to achieving emancipation. Those that involve longer term, almost lifelong planning, and those that are important when you finally start thinking about pulling the ripcord on your parachute and exiting out of working full time for someone else.

Many of the topics covered earlier in this book are fundamental to putting yourself in a position to be able to emancipate:

- You will need to determine if you can afford to emancipate from a financial standpoint…the "You Incorporated" chapters will help, and using the Rule of 72s can project when you will hit critical mass from a financial standpoint. As part of this, set some goals for how you plan to earn income after you emancipate and how much you expect to earn.

- Is your spouse or partner on board with your emancipation? Regularly discussing your goals, as covered early in the book, should help ensure you are both on the same page as you plan to enter this chapter of your lives.

- It's really important you think through what your typical day will look like after you emancipate. When you suddenly remove all the hours you've been putting in working for someone else your whole life, that can leave a pretty big void if you don't have a game plan for what you want to accomplish once you emancipate.

Use this book throughout your career

Here's the thing: no matter where you are in life, you can apply many of the concepts discussed in this book to stay on track with your life goals, which will help put you in a good position to emancipate when you're ready:

- Develop a habit to establish and regularly review your goals (as highlighted in Chapter 3) to make sure you are on track both on a short and long term basis.

- The Personal Inventory discussed in Chapter 4 can help keep you balanced, focused, and happy along the way as can the concepts discussed in Chapter 7: Is Stress an Issue for You?

- Managing your career to optimize your earnings and

advancement as first discussed in Chapter 6 and then again in Chapters 8 and 9 are key to generating adequate earnings over the course of your career.

- With your career properly launched and humming along, it's key to manage your income and ensure that you save and grow the savings consistently over time. This part of the process is covered in the "You Incorporated" Chapters 10-13 where you learn the basics of "Earning, Burning, and Churning" to build wealth along with a few basic but highly successful ways of putting your money to work.

Will there be a bigger impact if you apply all these things in your early 20's? Yes, no doubt there will be but even if you start these approaches in your 50's, it will help improve your position when the time comes to emancipate yourself…you just might be a little older by the time you're financially ready.

Are you ready to emancipate?

First, you need to determine, from a financial standpoint, can you sustain your desired post-emancipation lifestyle if you no longer have an income from working for someone else (or doing what you are currently doing for income).

How much will your post-emancipation lifestyle cost?

Going through all those details, which are different for each person, is beyond the scope of this book but here's the basics:

- You need to assess how much it will cost to support the post-emancipation lifestyle you desire.
    - Do you still have kids to put through school?
    - Do you still have a house to pay off?
    - Do you want to travel the world first class?

- Do you have a pension?
- When are you going to start taking social security?
- How will you cover healthcare expenses?
- Each of these elements, along with tracking your regular expenses vs your budget, will provide an idea of how much money you need to sustain yourself.

Projecting your nest egg and annual earnings potential

Once you've thought through how much your post-emancipation life will cost you per month or per year, you need to assess these costs against how much money you have in various investments.

- Based on the size of your nest egg, you can then estimate how much income, based on historic market performance, your investment portfolio should be able to generate each year.
    - For example: using the investments noted in Chapter 13, assuming at age 55 I had 2/3 of my portfolio in equity index funds and 1/3 in bonds, based on historic average performance, I could assume the equity portion would generate an average 10% annual return while the bonds would generate an average 3% annual return.
    - The weighted average return for that combined portfolio would be 7.6% (2/3 x 10%) + (1/3 x 3%), if past historic averages continue in the future.
    - If I have a portfolio worth $1 million at that point in time, I could estimate, on average, that it will generate about $76,000 per year in growth (7.6% x $1 million).
    - Furthermore, using the rule of 72s discussed in Chapter 11, you know that the 7.6% average return means your portfolio will double every 9.5 years (72/7.6% = 9.47 years).

- As a result, you know that in 10 years, at age 65, your portfolio (assuming you add no new savings) will double and likely be worth around $2 million and will be throwing off about $152,000 per year in annual returns.
- Hopefully you can see, by using these simple calculations, you can run these types of scenarios at any age to get a sense of where you are vs where you need to be to achieve magical emancipation. You would add to these numbers any other sources of income you have such as social security, a pension, etc.
- Once you have the amount of income you expect, you would compare that to your expected expenses to see how you would fare, keeping in mind the portfolio income shown above is an expected average: over the long term, this estimate is probably fairly accurate but it could vary significantly year to year. If you have more expected average annual income than costs, you can probably emancipate without touching your nest egg.

Life Hack #38: To be able to achieve emancipation or even to retire at the age of 65, you need to build financial critical mass over the course of your working life by saving regularly and investing prudently.

According to a 2019 survey by the Federal Reserve, the average retirement savings for Americans aged 50-59 was $160,000. Using this amount and the retirement example above, this average person would have their $160,000 invested 2/3 in a stock index fund and 1/3 in a bond index fund, the expected average return of 7.6% is only going to produce $12,160 per year. Unless you have a significant pension or other sources of income, you will be relying on social security to have any kind of reasonable retirement, so emancipation before you are eligible for social security is probably not realistic.

The above somewhat depressing example hopefully highlights what I've been preaching throughout this book. Use the tools in the "You Incorporated" chapters to build real wealth over the course of your career so you have options to do what you want, when you want, later in life.

My emancipation

I started the emancipation thought process in early 2020, before the pandemic hit. I was becoming less enthusiastic about continuing to do what I was doing for work. While I ostensibly had a good, reasonably high paying job as senior vice president for a global packaging company, it required a lot of travel and involved a fair amount of pressure and stress, and those aspects of my work life were getting pretty old and tiresome.

The starting point for my emancipation self assessment was a serious review of what I wanted to do with my life *after* working for someone else for so many years.

This is key: it seems to me, most folks who end up being bored or dissatisfied with their "retirement" have likely not spent enough time thoughtfully thinking about what they want to do with their lives ***before*** they pull the plug on working for someone else.

I thought long and hard about what I would potentially want to do after I emancipated, and I started to come up with several lists:

- What are specific things I want to accomplish-places I want to visit and other significant things I want to do?
- What are some things I potentially might want to do for "work" and to earn money, post-emancipation?
- What are the steps I need to go through to achieve emancipation…how do I get from where I was…still working..to actually exiting my job and emancipating?

- What are the critical expenses I need to cover post emancipation (such as healthcare) while living the life my wife and I want to live, and how do I determine a reasonable budget for these things?
- Where do we want to live after I emancipate and what's the cost to do that?

Bottom line: it was not a snap decision; where I got fed up with work and one day just quit!

Do I have the dinero?

Once I had spent a few months sorting through all of the above items, I had developed a decent idea of the range of monthly expenses I would likely have post emancipation. With this information in hand, I could then do a realistic review of whether or not I had enough money to carry out my emancipation plan.

The two things I think stop most people in their tracks when considering emancipation are:

1. The black hole of having to secure healthcare insurance prior to Medicare eligibility at age 65.
2. Being afraid their money won't last.

While these are both important, valid questions to ask before pulling the trigger on your plan, if you go through the process shown above, you should have the data you need to objectively determine if you can emancipate from a financial standpoint.

In my case, I had always tracked our budget and managed our investments myself, so I knew these numbers well and had a good feel for how our investment portfolio would likely grow over time based on past market performance. I thought through my options on when I would potentially begin drawing social security and the pension I have from a past employer.

With these income streams, the longer you wait, the higher the payout, so determining when you plan to start drawing on them impacts your calculations.

Time to think about your bucket list!

Onto this "current financial situation" information, I layered on specific things we wanted to do once I stopped working. For example, throughout our marriage we've always really enjoyed boating on the Great Lakes, and a major bucket list item we want to accomplish in the next few years is cruising America's Great Loop. This is an approximately 6,000 mile trip by water around the eastern half of the US. It can take anywhere from 6 months to several years, depending on how much time you want to spend along the way. In my financial assessment, I included the anticipated costs for this adventure along with our normal ongoing costs. So it's important you also try to factor in the costs of big things you want to accomplish in your life after you stop working for someone else.

I also factored in the likely cost of buying healthcare insurance for us. While this cost can be somewhat daunting given most folks rely on their employer's health insurance during their working years, the reality is you can buy health insurance. Yes, it's expensive and the available options are somewhat complicated to sort out, but it's just another expense, like your mortgage, that you simply have to include in the above calculations. If you can afford it, don't let it stop you from living your life!

Sensitivity check your numbers

With all these numbers in hand, I then "sensitivity checked" this against several potential future economic scenarios:

- What if the market flatlined over the next several years and it generated no return?
- Worse, what if the stock market craters by, say, 50% shortly after my retirement and it takes a few years to recover? Would

we have enough money not only to survive but also thrive, and still be able to do everything we want?

- After doing all of this carefully over the course of several months, I arrived at the definitive conclusion that yes (thankfully!), no matter how I sliced and diced the numbers, we had the money to live the life we wanted to and could survive any reasonable downturn just fine.

- Depending on your specific situation and how far away you are from emancipation, you might want to consider other potential variables such as other potential major expenses, your spouse's working plans, etc.

Here's an example of how this sensitivity analysis might look:

- Let's say, using all the tools covered in this book, you expect to have an investment portfolio of $5 million by the time you emancipate.

- Further, let's assume you expect to have a 60%40% portfolio allocation between equities and bonds at that time. That would mean you'd have $3 million in equities and $2 million in bonds/cash.

- Let's also say your expected annual expenses to live the life you want are expected to be $100,000.

- You know, using historical averages, this portfolio will throw off about $360,000 per year (10% of the $3 million equity portfolio is $300,000 plus 3% of the $2 million bond/cash portfolio is $60,000 for a total of $360,000 per year).

- To now consider a "worse case scenario" let's say the equity market collapses by 50% in a given year.

    - That would mean your $5 million portfolio gets cut to $3.5 million (now with $1.5 million in equities and still $2 million in bonds/cash).

    - Post crash, the equities go back to throwing off 10% per year, or $150,000, and the bond/cash keeps chugging along throwing off $60,000 per year. That is a total of $210,000 per year.

    - Granted, that's not as nice as the pre-crash $360,000 per year, but it's still more than double what you've determined you need to live the lifestyle you desire, which costs $100,000 per year.

- So, can you still afford to pull the plug and live the life you want even in this not so great scenario? Yes, you can and with money to spare. And here's the likely reality: usually (but not always) whenever equity markets crash in one year, they roar back hard over the next few years. So, as long as you don't get frightened and pull your money out of the market when it crashes (locking in your losses permanently), and you let that equity portfolio continue to ride, the likelihood is that $1.5 million balance will probably bounce back much more than 10% per year following the crash.

Don't get hung up on the dollars I used in the above example... Whether your portfolio is $5 million or $500,000 or $50,000...the point is, you are determining how much you need to live your life the way you want and how much of a portfolio you will need to support that lifestyle.

The beauty of this thought process is that you can do it at any stage of your working life to see if your life dreams are aligning with your financial reality...**and if needed, you can course correct to change the road you are on.**

Yes, you have the dinero!

Completing this thought process and analysis is a huge checkmark on the road to emancipation. Once done, you have a good idea of what you want to do both generally and with some specifics after emancipation and you know, if you stay the course on your earning, burning, and churning, you will have the dough to weather any likely storm and still be in good shape. Having the peace of mind that the money will be there can really help free you to fully enjoy your emancipation.

What if the numbers don't add up or I don't have a plan?

If you go through this process and find you don't really know what you want to do with your life post emancipation, and/or you don't have the money to live the life you want to, then you must go back to the drawing board and figure out how you want to proceed:

- To address the financial piece, you can, for example, change how you're saving and spending, or you can work longer to better reposition yourself for success post-emancipation.
- Beyond the finances, what's really important is you and your spouse jointly determining what you want to do in your post-emancipation life. It's a huge gift…make the most of it!
- Until you know with some specificity what you want to do and how you are going to fund that life, you're not ready.

Do you have the right emancipation mindset?

It's funny, but I think most people look at the prospect of retiring/emancipating the wrong way: they go into the process with the negative mindset of trying to figure out if they will run out of money.

I look at it differently: my goal, even now that I am emancipated, is to continually grow and build wealth. Even though I am now emancipated, I want to continue investing smartly and living within our means so that on average, our nest egg continues to grow while still allowing my wife and I to do all the things we want.

Your mindset here, as it is with most important things in life, is crucial. Don't go into emancipation worrying about if your money will run out and you'll be forced out into the streets begging for crumbs. Instead, go into emancipation looking to continue growing, evolving, and building on all aspects of your life, including your wealth. Granted, with my work income dropping off this year, the rate of my wealth building will decrease, but my goal is still to always be growing my wealth.

Life Hack #39: Take ownership of your financial and investment decisions...the earlier in life, the better. Doing so will give you much more confidence when you come to make critical decisions, such as when you can afford to emancipate, later in life. In addition to the massive cost savings over the course of your life that you get by choosing to do you own investing, you won't be relying on some advisor you pay to give you his or her blessing that it's ok for you to retire.

The exit plan

I spent many months thinking through my financial and post-emancipation plans. Once done, I was confident I was ready and able to pull the rip cord. At that point, I then had to determine the optimal way and timing to exit my full time work situation. Where I last worked, I had to consider my 401k vesting period as well as when various incentive programs would be paid out. To the extent I could coordinate my exit to maximize these things, so much the better. When you approach emancipation, it's also important for you to consider any incentive programs that could help maximize your financial situation before departing.

I was able to work out an exit plan with the person who ran the business I worked for so that I was able to help them properly transition our customers with minimal disruption while at the same time allowing me to optimize any incentives that were due. By being forthright and working constructively, I was able to achieve my exit in the timeframe I desired while helping ensure the company was not left in the lurch when I exited. It was a win/win for both parties and, in its own way, one final career "inflection point."

Emancipation game planning

As the time approached for my exit, I worked to outline some specific things I actually wanted to do with my post-emancipation time. I ended up with a daily game plan (written down of course) that would help me get after some of the important things I wanted to accomplish:

- One of the things I wanted to reprioritize was focusing more on the physical aspect of My Personal Inventory. While I've always been active, playing tennis, walking, and doing some exercises, my younger son developed a 4-day/week workout schedule for me using weights and machines. It's a great plan that I now do religiously along with all of my past ways of exercising, and I really enjoy it.

- I also wanted to finish writing this book which, as you can see, has now been accomplished.

- I wanted to get back to playing the guitar, an instrument I haven't really touched in many years.

- I also wanted to develop some expertise on the crypto markets, which I've also been rapidly learning over the past several months, as hopefully is shown in chapter 15.

- As discussed, the main source of my ongoing income is my investments and, with more time available, I wanted to optimize my investment returns focusing more regular time on this activity each day.

- I also wanted to consult on a fractional/project basis where my experience can add value.

Emancipation launch

I ended up with an ideal daily plan where I allocate targeted time each day to all of the above activities. I'm most productive in the morning, so I typically try to allocate 3-4 hours most mornings to work on each of these objectives. Do I work on all of these things exactly to my defined plan every day? No, I most certainly do not. But do I work on each of these things each week? Yes, I do. Well, other than guitar...I am hoping to allocate more time to it in the coming months now that this book has been completed!

As a result, I find I get up each morning with enthusiasm to tackle pieces of each of the above objectives, and then I have the rest of the day to "have fun." Some days, I really get into writing and, before I know it, hours have passed. Other days, the investing side is more appealing to me and I'll spend a few hours listening to various YouTube videos or podcasts from experts in the financial realm. I also started journaling, which I find helps summarize what I'm doing, how I'm feeling, and if my game plan needs adjustment.

While my somewhat fanatical approach to my emancipation may not be needed or right for everyone, thinking through all of this really helped me formulate some meaningful, productive activities, so when I did actually emancipate on April 30, 2021, the following Monday I was ready to go with a game plan of constructive things I wanted to work on.

I get a lot of satisfaction from these various activities. None of it seems like work and I've never sat around, bored and wondering what I want to do with my life because I thought through all of that pretty carefully before pulling the plug. Now, every day is full and I can honestly say I've not missed my pre-emancipation work life one nanosecond...so far. Could that change down the road? Sure, and if it does, what's the worst that can happen? Maybe I decide to do something different. From my perspective, it's all good, no matter what.

Other possibilities...

The work world is changing for the better. One of the silver linings coming out of the pandemic is workers of all stripes now have more clout in many ways than they did before the pandemic. Companies now know with a high degree of certainty that remote work is as productive as onsite work and, frankly, not keeping all that expensive office space is more efficient and flexible for many companies.

Fractional management

New ways of working continue to emerge as well. One of these, called fractional management, is one of the areas I'm exploring currently. What's a fractional manager? It's an experienced manager/executive who helps companies (often small or mid-size companies) on either a recurring part time basis (for example, 2 days per month with a retainer) or on an interim, full time basis (say three-six months while the company reloads a permanent executive for the role). This sparks my interest because what I've found I enjoyed in my last few full time roles and where I add the most value is at companies that are in transition or in a crisis. Those types of situations often overlap and are where there is a need for a fractional manager/leader. We'll see how it goes!

There are also a whole range of consulting/temporary and part time gigs out there for workers at all stages of their careers. Many of these gigs can be undertaken from anywhere in the world as long as you have a decent internet connection. Over the last several months, I've been doing 1-2 hour consulting gigs on a weekly basis through several consulting companies who match up expertise with businesses that need that expertise. These are often private equity firms looking to gain insight into a particular market or industry. Typically, in these arrangements, you set your own hourly rate which, depending on your experience, can be many hundreds of dollars per hour.

From my viewpoint, this is all a beautiful new day for work possibilities for both young and old alike…all it takes is thinking outside the box and imagining ways you can add value in whatever type of role you seek. These new ways of working offer the possibility of being emancipated throughout your career, not just when you approach typical "retirement" age.

Transitioning from *minimizing taxes* to *managing Income:*

One of the interesting aspects encountered when you achieve emancipation is your mindset as it relates to income and taxes. Given the massive numbers of baby boomers retiring on a daily basis, which was turbocharged during the pandemic (known as "The Great Resignation"), it's surprising there is not more written on this topic, but it's important when you enter the emancipation stage that you think through how you will manage your income.

When you are working, the game is all about minimizing taxes, which largely involves deferring income by using IRAs, 401ks, HSAs, and other methods. If you've been successful in building wealth through your career, you'll likely arrive at the emancipation stage with a significant amount of your net worth in IRAs and 401ks. In addition, if you earned a significant amount annually during your later working years, you were likely excluded, like I was, from being able to contribute to a Roth IRA because your income was too high.

When you go from significant working income one year to essentially no income the next year, you need to change your objective from minimizing each year's taxes to ***minimizing taxes over the remainder of your life***. That, in turn, could lead you to the conclusion to actually *create* taxable income by converting some of your non-Roth IRA and 401k assets into a Roth IRA.

This is because, at some point down the road (currently 72 years old), you will be required to take what's called Required Minimum Distributions (RMD) each year from all your non-Roth IRA and 401k plans. If you have a significant amount accumulated in these plans, your taxable income will likely hockey stick up at that point in time.

When you add your future RMD to your social security and pension income that you may be receiving at that time, you could find yourself in a pretty high tax bracket...certainly 22% or 24% or higher. And, let's be honest, in the current climate, tax rates are likely to go up in the future, not down, so your rate could be much higher at that time.

Compare that bleak tax prospect in your golden years to the years immediately after you emancipate. If you are like me and not planning to collect pension or social security until at least age 67, you may have very little income in the years immediately following emancipation. **For the first time in your adult life, you can control your income and, therefore, your tax rate.**

For example, at the time of this writing in early 2022, a married couple can earn $83,550 and still be in the 12% federal tax bracket. You can also capture capital gains and pay 0% tax if your total income is below this level. When you add the married standard deduction of $25,900, this means you can earn about $109,450 and pay about $9,300 in tax or 8.8% of your gross income in federal tax.

With those facts in mind, the question you have is, do you enjoy paying no income tax now but then, at age 72, you may have to start paying potentially 3 times that tax rate or more when you start having to take your RMDs? Or, instead, do you start converting some of the assets out of your non-Roth IRA and 401ks into a Roth IRA and lock in the lower tax rate now, even though that forces you to pay more taxes now?

When your income is low, it can be really smart to take advantage of the lower tax brackets with a Roth conversion and/or the zero % capital gains rate if you have some stocks you would like to sell that have appreciated. That's my current game plan: Each year until I start taking social security and my pension at age 67, I plan to capture capital gains and convert funds from IRA and 401k accounts to my Roth IRA up to the point that my income maxes out the 12% tax bracket which again, is currently $109,450 assuming the standard deduction for a married couple is taken. I'd rather shell out the taxes now at an average 8.8% rate and have the money converted into the Roth grow tax free forever than not pay the taxes now and pay at least 22% when I have to start taking RMDs in my early 70's.

Social Security and pension choices

You and your spouse are likely entitled to receive social security benefits at some point and, potentially, you may have a pension you can draw on in the future. Both social security and pension monthly payouts increase dramatically if you can hold off on starting to receive these benefits. Each person is different, but if you have the resources to not have to tap into social security and/or your pension immediately, you should consider delaying collecting these income streams and save those lifetime income streams for later in order to maximize this guaranteed monthly income for the rest of your life.

Life Hack #40: Approaching retirement or emancipation, as I refer to it, requires some thoughtful consideration on both the financial and personal side. In my opinion, both are equally important: you need to really determine what you want to accomplish with this gift of available time. The outcome of that thought process, to some extent, will dictate how many dollars you will need to support your future life.

Look at the financial side in a sober, objective way:

- **What's your budget going to be?**
- **What realistic return will your portfolio generate under different market return assumptions?**
- **Don't let the healthcare cost "black hole" scare you away…it's a cost like your mortgage or any other major expense you will have to fund if you emancipate before being Medicare eligible.**

Thinking through these elements before you pull the cord on your permanent job will hopefully allow you to move forward without the stress of "will I run out of money?"

Financial adjustments transitioning into emancipation:
Much like the major expenditures flagged in Step 2 of Chapter 12, I've gone into my emancipation with the mind set that I want to always have 2-3 years of annual living expenses held in cash (in a bank or money market account) in order to ride out any significant market ups and downs. For example, if your annual budget is $100,000, you would want $200-300k in cash to cover your expected living expenses and you would want to maintain that level throughout your retirement.

There are some "rules of thumb" financial professionals advise for determining how much of your portfolio you can "afford to spend" each year to help ensure you don't run out of money in retirement. These rules would generally tell you that you should not spend more than 3-4% of your portfolio each year, adjusted for inflation, to give you high odds your money will last throughout your life.

Using the $5 million portfolio used in the earlier example, and following this guidance, you would enter retirement planning to spend 3-4% of this amount, or $150-200k in the first year. You would then adjust that amount for each year's inflation rate in the future.

While this 3-4% guideline has some usefulness, my issue is that this approaches the problem from the wrong angle: these rules assume you simply don't want to run out of money, rather than assuming you want to continue to **grow** your wealth into the future. Far better, in my view, is to follow my approach and determine what you want to do with your post-emancipation life and how much money it will cost to support, then build a 2-3 year reserve in order to weather any market-induced storms. To the extent your annual spending amount is less than what average return your portfolio generates, that excess will support growing your wealth.

Chapter 17

Conclusion & Final Thoughts

There's a funny Albert Brooks/Meryl Streep movie called "Defending Your Life" where the premise is Albert's character needs to defend his life in order to earn entry into heaven after his death. The big thing he's defending is whether or not he lived his life without too much fear.

It's a valid point...we do tend to live our lives in more fear than is often healthy and this can lead us to not taking the chances we should to live a full, rewarding life. I've certainly been guilty of that and have some regrets not taking chances on business ideas earlier in my career that maybe I should have.

Other than the learning to be gained though, there's not a lot of value in looking back and dwelling on the mistakes of the past too much. Better to forge ahead, trying to live your life to the fullest. As I often say to my kids and others who will listen: "suck the life out of every day." You never know how many you have left!

Along with trying to avoid dwelling too much on the past, I think it's important to watch out for your own rationalizations on what's not working in your life: whether that is with respect to your fitness, your relationships, or your career success. As noted several times in this book, **you own you**.

The sooner you face the reality of the key aspects of your own life in an objective way, and don't view all of your shortcomings as the result of fate, genetics, or being the victim of something or someone else, the sooner you can start the exciting work of achieving your full potential. You'll also be setting a good example for others such as your spouse and kids, which in turn might help them on their journey.

A final thought is to keep an eye out for those "God Winks." Often, in the hustle and bustle and chaos we often allow our daily lives to become, it's easy to miss the gentle nudges that are out there to help move us in the right direction. It takes work to live in the moment, to be aware of the blessings we all have, and to be open to the opportunities that are often flashing all around us. There are ways to help open our minds to these possibilities, including prayer and meditation, but this is an individual journey where I think each person must find their own way. The next challenge is when you get the God Wink, insight, or whatever you choose to call it, do you have the courage and conviction to listen and follow it? But that's a topic and discussion for another book!

After many years of starts and stops on this writing effort, I have a sense of accomplishment in having completed this book. My true hope is that the things I've recounted here are helpful in some way to you, whether it be the Personal Inventory to help keep daily life on track and in balance, or the basic financial discussion provided later in the book.

As I look back on my journey thus far, the two accomplishments I'm most proud of **are not** my original goals of becoming a VP by 33 or a millionaire by 40. The two that are most important are first, having had an impact on raising two confident, happy sons who are pursuing their passions and are morally good, sensible young adults.

Second, by utilizing the "Personal Inventory" described in Chapter 4 to help get me through my sometimes challenging, early teen years as well as "My Mantra" described in Chapter 7 that helped navigate the stressful challenges of my mid-20's, these tools really helped me achieve the ultimate goal of sustained happiness during the vast majority of my adult life. And I'm still very happy today.

It's my hope that some or all of these tools will be helpful to you in your life's journey. It's easy to get sucked into the angst of the current time we live in with one crisis it seems like following the other, and the talking points of our "leaders" always seeming to be organized to pit one group of people against the other. I choose not to get sucked into all that.

To me, this is a golden age of opportunity for those that seek to pursue it. There have never been lower barriers to starting a global business utilizing the technology that is within the grasp and financial means of most folks. It's also never been easier to access training for new skills. Finally, there has never been a better time when average people can access excellent financial investment options at minimal cost. So, rather than wasting a single moment stressing about the current or next crisis that comes along (you can be certain there will always be one!), turn off the news and social media feeds and take advantage of these opportunities and live ***your*** life to the fullest and happiest extent possible.

I welcome your thoughts...especially if there is something in this book you have found useful or if you have some advice for me (be nice and, sorry, there are no refunds!). Feel free to email me at thrivindude@yahoo.com. Also, check out my website, thrivinllc.com.

Acknowledgements

Whew! I am really happy to be publishing this book after so many years. I couldn't have completed it without the input and motivation provided by my long time business associate and sometimes recruiter Russ Riendeau. Russ is one of those rare renaissance guys who runs marathons, writes poetry, composes music, and writes books…all in his spare time while being one of the best recruiters in the business. Thanks for all your valuable insight Russ!

Also, I appreciate all the kind help, as a newbie writer, from Daria Lacy. She did a great job doing the layout and graphic design as well as helping me shepherd the book to publication.

My older son Dallas provided helpful insight on the writing and publishing process from his experience as a writer, and my younger son Dylan helped sanity check the You Incorporated chapters and lent his expertise for the Crypto chapter of the book.

Finally, a big thanks to Cathy, my wife of now 35 years, for not only putting up with me all these years but also for her help in the final copy editing for the book.

Selected References & Suggested Resources

Be a learning creature! Always be working to improve your mind and learn new things...your life will be richer in many ways as a result. The following are either books I've referenced in this book or resources that might be helpful to the reader in learning more about some of the topics covered.

First, proper attribution for the lyrics quoted in the book:
Chapter 5: Lyric from "Stairway to Heaven" written by Jimmy Page and Robert Plant and performed by Led Zeppelin. Originally released in 1971 on the band's untitled fourth studio album dubbed by fans "Led Zeppelin IV." The album was released on Atlantic Records.

Chapter 7: Lyric from "Changes" written and performed by David Bowie. Originally released in 1971 on Bowie's album Hunky Dory. The album was released on RCA Records.

Books:
The Real Anthony Fauci: Bill Gates, Big Pharma, and the Global War on Democracy and Public Health (2021) by Robert F. Kennedy, Jr. Mark Twain once sagely observed that it's much easier to fool someone than it is to convince them that they've been fooled. That is certainly the case with the recent pandemic. Whether you've been obediently following everything the government has been telling you since February of 2020 or you've suspected there is more at play than our government's altruistic best intentions for our safety, this well researched book, with over 2,200 footnotes, will wake you up and potentially piss you off when you understand what is really behind the global Covid strategy.

Perks and Parachutes: Negotiating Your Best Possible Employment Deal (1985 and updated in 1997) by John Tarrant with Paul Fargis. There are probably other awesome resources on this topic now, but when I made my first big career move in 1997 from being VP at the company I started out of college with to a new VP role at a new company in a new industry, this was the book I used to figure out how to negotiate and structure my best deal. I've continued to refer to this book ever since. If nothing else, this book makes you aware of what the possible negotiation elements are including compensation, signing bonuses, and the important but often overlooked exit compensation agreement.

Getting to Yes: Negotiating Agreements Without Giving In (1981 and updated in 1991 and 2011) by Roger Fisher and William Ury Very readable with concepts that are understandable and easy to apply in your everyday life.

Outliers: The Story of Success (2008) by Malcolm Gladwell. A fantastic writer who turns somewhat mundane topics into highly interesting reading. This book highlights why it's important that each of us "get our 10,000 hours in" if we want to be really expert at what we choose to do.

The Little Book of Common Sense Investing: The Only Way to Guarantee Your Fair Share of Stock Market Returns (2017) by Jack Bogle. Jack Bogle did more to raise the wealth of average Americans than any politician or government program with his invention of the index mutual fund. Any book by him is worth a read if you want to improve your financial literacy.

The Sovereign Individual: Mastering the Transition to the Information Age (1999) by James Dale Davidson & Lord William Rees Mogg. The amount of stuff these guys anticipated in the late 90's that has actually occurred so far is mind-blowing. What they project that is yet to come is even more exciting. What I want to know is why they haven't written anything more in the past 20 years on these topics!

When God Winks: How the Power of Coincidence Guides Your Life (2018) by Squire Rushnell. In my opinion, it's hard to find true happiness in life without a significant spiritual component. This book helps you identify when God is trying to nudge you along in the right direction. The trick is listening!

You are the Placebo: Making Your Mind Matter (2015) by Dr. Joe Dispenza. A remarkable true story which makes the case that ***we*** are truly the masters of our physical and emotional health and, not generally, modern medicine.

Your Money or Your Life: 9 Steps to Transforming Your Relationship with Money and Achieving Financial Independence (2018) by Vicki Robin & Joe Dominguez. This book altered my path in life and provided a lot of the foundation for my recent emancipation. This is the book that ignited the whole FIRE (Financially Independent Retire Early) movement over the past 20+ years.

The Four Hour Workweek: Escape the 9-5, Live Anywhere, and Join the New Rich (2009) by Timothy Ferriss. This book was well ahead of its time. Tim also has an excellent podcast, The Tim Ferriss Show, that covers a broad range of interesting people and topics such as health, wellness, and finance.

Other Resources I find interesting and useful:

Investments:
Listed below are a few websites for good, low cost investment companies. There are many others, but these three are among the largest and most well established. Each website provides a wealth of free information on investing for you to learn more.

Fidelity: Fidelity.com

Charles Schwab: Schwab.com

Vanguard: Vanguard.com

Paying Off Debt:
Dave Ramsey: Ramseysolutions.com. Dave Ramsey has a syndicated radio show, a website, and offers classes focused on escaping the evil trap debt can become for many people.

Crypto:
Anthony Pompliano's YouTube channel provides great insight and the latest on crypto and the evolving metaverse.

Coin Bureau's YouTube channel also provides great education in easy to understand language on all things crypto.

Expat Life...Living the Sovereign Individual life:

The **Nomad Capitalist** YouTube channel provides excellent insight on options and ways to consider expanding your citizenship options beyond where you currently reside.

International Living has been the go-to magazine for decades in learning where and how to live in other parts of the world from a practical standpoint. Great writing from people who are actually doing it. Once our Great Loop adventure is completed, we plan on striking out to live in several other countries around the world for extended periods of time and this magazine has been a great resource to plan those adventures.

Perspective on real time events:

Joe Rogan's podcasts on Spotify, which are also excerpted on YouTube, provide non-mainstream insight and commentary on what is going on in the world today…often without Big Brother's stamp of approval on the content, which is quite refreshing.

Russell Brand's YouTube channel also provides really interesting and frequently funny commentary on what is going on in the world today from an objective and thoughtful perspective.

Investing: The **Valuetainment** YouTube channel covers a broad range of topics including business and investing as well as broader current event topics.

America's Great Loop:

If I've sparked an interest to learn more about America's Great Loop, the American Great Loop Cruisers Association (AGLCA) is an excellent resource which has a number of good videos on their YouTube channel **Great Loop**.

Made in the USA
Monee, IL
04 November 2026

67385471R00125